DIE
DAILY

DIE

DAILY

DREAM, IMPROVE, ENJOY

By

TED LENNOX
Editor: NINA DERDA

Order this book online at www.trafford.com
or email orders@trafford.com

Most Trafford titles are also available at major online book retailers.

Note for Librarians: A cataloguing record for this book is available from Library
and Archives Canada at www.collectionscanada.ca/amicus/index-e.html

Printed in Victoria, BC, Canada.

ISBN: 978-1-4269-1133-0

*Our mission is to efficiently provide the world's finest, most comprehensive book publishing
service, enabling every author to experience success. To find out how to publish your book, your
way, and have it available worldwide, visit us online at www.trafford.com*

Trafford rev. 9/21/2009

Trafford
PUBLISHING®   www.trafford.com

North America & international
toll-free: 1 888 232 4444 (USA & Canada)
phone: 250 383 6864 ♦ fax: 812 355 4082

ACKNOWLEDGEMENTS

Tribute to Nina Derda

Nina has helped me write this book,
Please understand she took more than a look.
Her thoughts and suggestions were oh so kind,
They all were meant to stimulate my mind!

Her thoughts, ideas, and suggestions were meant to inspire,
They always helped me raise my expectations higher.
In my life she's been a positive catalyst,
Encourages me to think sunshine and ignore the mist!

Nina has helped me keep this book so clear,
To always be myself without any fear.
What you'll read is just plain me,
Nina encouraged my complete honesty!

I thank Nina for help in keeping me straight.
She says, "Ted, just be yourself." For me her counsel was great!
The message from Nina that I do perceive,
Is to believe in myself and thus I'll achieve.

I'm saying thanks for Nina's super support,

But, "thanks" is a word that falls far short.

In a way for this book there are authors two,

I aspire to give Nina the credit she's due!

Nancy Kimberlin and John Whitacre

Throughout the writing of this book my friend John has encouraged me and provided much guidance. In fact, John connected me with the Trafford Publishing Company. As you read this book, you will find out how important tactile pictures are for people who are blind. Thus, in this book there will be four pictures. John's daughter Nancy has kindly done the visual drawings for my book. Nancy enthusiastically took my tactile drawings and converted them most effectively into print drawings for the print copy of this volume.

I am grateful to both Nancy and John for their support, interest, and for the drawings that enhance my book. There will also be a Braille version.

I want to thank John's daughter, her name is Nancy.

She has helped make this book quite fancy.

When off to school her kiddies did leave,

These pictures she drew to help me achieve.

John has been an important part

Of my book since the day I did start.

His advice has kept me on the right route.

And he helped my mind to keep away from doubt!

PREFACE

I WILL START WITH A
MESSAGE FROM MY HEART

This is a poetry book. However, I have included a fair amount of autobiographical information. The autobiographical material is used mainly to introduce, explain, and amplify my poetry. It is my hope that this will add understanding, insight, and enjoyment. As you read and reflect it is my honest hope that you will feel that you know me and are comfortable in my presence.

I included my e-mail address at the end of Chapter One and on the back cover of the book. If you have an urge or a desire to communicate with me, I'd be delighted. Further, I promise I will respond to all messages.

Please enjoy <u>DIE Daily</u>—please reflect on a poem occasionally; please smile and chuckle every once in a while; and please know that everything from this moment on is meant to be positive, inspiring, joyful, and or humorous.

I cannot resist sharing the following nifty notions—these nifty notions apply to me and may or may not apply to anyone else. There are three different ways I enjoy reading poetry:

1. I really relish reading poetry out loud.

2. I love listening to others read poetry aloud.

3. I find delight in reading poems using my fingers. In other words, reading them in braille.

INTERESTING WORDS

There are four words in this book that I feel a need to define or explain. I've chosen these four words because prior to writing these poems I had never used them before and perhaps a few of you will not be familiar with them either. It is my desire to communicate clearly with each of you, ergo, in order for that to happen each word must be meaningful.

The first word is in Chapter Ten, "OUR DANCE WITH ROMANCE." The word is in the poem, "AMPUTATED YET MOTIVATED." The word I am talking about is, "TROGLODYTE." As used here, it means "to become seclusive and withdrawn". The second word is in Chapter Eleven, "WE ARE NOW CAUGHT WITH A LITTLE AFTERTHOUGHT." The word there is, "ERGO." It simply means "therefore". The next word is also in Chapter Eleven and it is, "POTPOURRI." In this case it is meant to mean "a collection of various items". Then, the fourth word is somewhere in this book. If it isn't, I'll find a place for it. The word is one I like a lot; it is positive and it is fun to say aloud. It is, "SALUBRIOUS." It basically means "healthy and good looking". When I want to flatter someone - mainly ladies - I accuse them of being salubrious!

In the process of reading Chapter Six I discovered two more words that I think need defining. They are in the poem, "SYMPHONIC

LIVING." a poem I am devoted to. The first word is "SONOROUS." Within the poem it means "to have a pleasant sound - to be pleasant and peaceful". The next word is "CACOPHONIC" and is used to mean "unpleasant and out of harmony".

So here are the six words I'm drawing to your attention:

- ☼ *Troglodyte*
- ☼ *Ergo*
- ☼ *Potpourri*
- ☼ *Salubrious*
- ☼ *Sonorous*
- ☼ *Cacophonic*

Table of Contents

WELCOME TO MY POETRY RIVER
I HOPE THAT I DO DELIVER

THIS DAY

I start each and every day,
In a positive and joyful way,
Today as I throw back the sheet,
This day I'm exuberant to greet!

Every morning as I put my feet on the floor,
Internally I shout, "Life! It's you I adore!"
So today I get up with joy in my heart,
Eagerly ready for this day to start!

I welcome the sun, the snow, and the breeze,
Inside me I'm warm and I never will freeze,
I think thoughts that lead me to achieve,
For in myself I've learned to believe!

Ted Lennox

Greetings to whoever dares to read some or all of my poetry. If you have the courage and the determination to read through some or all my poems, I hope that you will find them interesting, inspiring, enjoyable, humorous, and of value. Different poems have different purposes. For instance, my poem GOLF in the chapter HUMOR OR RUMOR simply lets you know what a great golfer I am!!! (:-)

By golly, since this book is a book of poetry, let's launch it with a poem that has been part of me ever since I read it in 1975. That's 33 years ago. I read it in the monthly publication entitled Daily Word. Interestingly, it was the first copy of Daily Word I ever received. Could it have been a case of Divine Timing? The poem is written by Viola Lukaweicki. It was and is an important poem with a FANTASTIC message—at least for me. Happily, it came at a most difficult time in my life. Thanks, Viola!

Okay, Ted, ole boy, get to the second poem. Jeepers! It tickles me to think that the second poem is not one of mine. That tells you how much this poem means to me.

REALITY
By Viola Lukaweicki

My thoughts are very potent things,

They hem me in or give me wings,

My thoughts create, enslave, or free,

Enrich or impoverish me!

My own thoughts make me glad or sad,

They choose decide for good or bad,

Whate're they be is true for me,

My thoughts are my reality!

Introducing Myself

The name I go by is Ted Lennox. When I was growing up my family and friends called me T. R., except my dad, who called me Ribs. Later, as a young man and to tease my brothers Frank and Cecil, I called myself Tough and Rough. Perhaps you will read my poem about the importance of names. It is part of Chapter 3 entitled, "TO COMMUNICATE IS REALLY GREAT!"

I am now retired from teaching. I had a rather short career as a teacher. After a brief 47.6 years I retired at the youthful age of 71. Most of those years, I was happily engaged in teaching children who were blind or had low vision. I now have students all over our country working, raising families, paying taxes, and living exciting lives. By the way, for many years my students called me Mr. OBG. You may wonder what OBG stands for. It's "Old, Bald and Gray." Just so you know, there's not a word of truth in it!

Since I myself am blind I must mention that blindness is simply an inconvenience. I hope that I encouraged my students to dream big, and then to work with vigor and confidence to make those dreams a reality.

My wife Laura and I have just celebrated our 45th wedding anniversary. We have two wonderful daughters who have provided us with two great sons-in-law. Now, joy of joys, we have Dave, Emma, Anna, Sarah, Naomi, Brittany, and Cody. I'll let you guess who they are. I will tell you that they range in age from one year to twelve years old.

When I proposed to Laura, I promised her a boring life. On our 40th anniversary she turned to me and impishly quipped: "By the way, Ted, when does this boring life that you promised me begin?" God has blessed us both richly.

As you know, I have entitled this book <u>DIE Daily: Dream, Improve, Enjoy.</u>

Chapter 2 will amplify the meaning of the title.

Please read my poems, enjoy them, and maybe think about them. Preceding the poems I have written short, and I hope interesting, commentaries about them. In addition, some of the poems have drawings that accompany them. This, I hope will add interest.

Further, you might find it exciting to know that this book will also be published in braille, and the pictures will be raised so that they convey meaning to the fingers. Tactile pictures are just as valuable and enriching as are visual pictures. Tactile drawings are not duplicates of visual drawings because the fingers process information in a different way than do the eyes. However, meaningful pictures that a blind child or person can touch are so, so important. I would like to get on my soap box and tell you much more about the importance of meaningful drawings for the blind, and how they need to be done. However, this is a poetry book so let's proceed to Chapter 2. The theme of this chapter will amplify and clarify the title of this book—namely, DIE Daily. Send me an e-mail and tell me what you think if you wish. I would enjoy hearing from you! My e-mail address is: tedlennox@ gmail.com. Congratulations! You managed to make it through the first 943 words.

CHAPTER

2

DAILY I DIE
THAT I DO TRY

Dream, Improve, Enjoy

Now that Viola has gotten us off to a resounding start I shall introduce you to three important poems. Please, if you don't mind, as you read them give them a little thought. Perhaps they will speak a bit to you, to your children, or grandchildren. I will amiably admit that they speak to me, and this coming year Dave, age 13, and Emma, age 10, will have at least one of these poems in their birthday card. Moreover, we will have an interesting discussion about the poem. And thanks to you, my reader, as I write this to you, I have easily decided that this year's card will include the poem that represents the letter D in my acronym—DIE! As you know, the D stands for DREAM.

Okay, here are the three poems that will reveal more about why I titled the book DIE Daily.

DREAM

My advice to myself and maybe you'll agree,
Is to DIE daily; it'll set you free!
It's a three letter word, the first letter is D.
The D stands for dream. Please listen to me.

Take time to dream every single day,
That's so important, that's what I say!
So take time to dream, it will enrich your life,
Let your mind soar, take time out from strife,

Take time each day to put your head in a cloud,
Of this time you can surely be proud,
Dream away and don't delay,
This should be part of our every day!

I am writing this on my wonderful BrailleNote. After inserting this poem into Chapter 2, I listened to my BrailleNote read it aloud to me. Then, I read the poem again to myself using the braille display. I didn't just read it; I am sitting quietly by myself in my living room, and so, I read it aloud. Although I would like to keep writing, I'm not going to do that. Guess what I shall do right now! I am going to set aside fifteen minutes or so simply to dream, to meditate, and spend a little quality time with myself. Be back in the near future.

I believe that I have carefully conveyed the notion to you that for me dreaming is important. Please note the two words "for me." In no way do I wish to speak for anyone else but myself. We each should decide whether dreaming is important or not. However, I would suggest to teachers that it might be prudent to spend a little time each week in their classrooms allowing and encouraging their students to dream. If I were to go back to the classroom, I'd set a little time aside each week for my students and their teacher to dream away.

We now have laid a fabulous foundation for our lives. What's the next step in Dieing Daily? Ah yes! Start putting some of those dreams into practice. That brings us to the second element, or second poem in this chapter, namely, "IMPROVE." Putting it simply, ideally we should be better today than we were yesterday; and we should be better tomorrow than we are today. Wow! What a great dream; what a dandy goal. Here we go forward to the poem that represents the second letter in our acronym; the letter I.

IMPROVE

As long as one is still alive,

Improvement is something for which to strive,

A person 'til death should always be growing,

The garden of life is meant for hoeing!

Live your life in a positive groove,

Keep it exciting with your every move,

Always keep striving to improve.

Dream, improve, every twenty-four,

To DIE each day there's something more!

The letter E we must now explore,

So go to part three to open that door.

ENJOY

The three letters DIE is an acronym,

Taken together they fill life with vim.

The letter D tells us to dream,

Improving is the I - it's part of the scheme!

But what is the letter E you may wonder?

It fills one's life with lightning and thunder.

Listen to this and this is no PLOY!

Make each moment, a moment to ENJOY!!!

DIE daily is my cry,

This, each day do I try,

Dream, improve, and please enjoy,

This might be a motto for each girl and boy!

The title of this book is now perfectly clear. You might think the name DIE Daily is misleading, and it is if taken literally. However, it is meant as an open invitation to live and to live with direction, enthusiasm, and joy. So off we go to Chapter 3, "TO COMMUNICATE IS REALLY GREAT!" It is my hope that you will find some poems to smile about and some poems that will cause you to think just a bit about the process and the importance of communicating clearly.

CHAPTER

3

TO COMMUNICATE
IS REALLY GREAT

It is awesome to me to think about communicating with others. First, the ability to communicate with words is fantastic! Words are wonderful when used kindly, clearly, and caringly. Of course, it is like anything else in the world, words can be used for good or for bad. In this book the purpose of words is to bring human beings together in harmony, peace, and mutual support.

Words, however, are not the only means by which we communicate. Let me list a few more. Touch. Read and reflect upon my next poem which I named, simply, "THE IMPORTANCE OF TOUCH." Then there is the power of a smile or the opposite, the power of a frown. Tone of voice - what an important aspect of communication! The final element of communication is that of posture - it can convey much.

What to heck! I'm making the kick-off poem for this chapter my poem on touch.

Ted Lennox

THE IMPORTANCE OF TOUCH

We communicate in many a-way,
Our messages so to convey,
Let's take a look at how we say,
Our thoughts and feelings every day!

If you're smiling or if you frown,
You tell me you're in the pink or in the brown,
The messages you convey with your face,
Will tell me to approach or stay in my place!

You tell me so much by the tone of your voice,
The tone you select is a personal choice.
Just express a bit of joy with your every greeting,
What a treat you provide for the person you're meeting!

Yes, even your posture signals your mood,
It says you're happy or feeling crude,
Sit up straight and be interested in life,
Not slouched over and communicating strife!

One purpose of this poem is to talk about touch,
To so many many people it can say so much,
A gentle tap upon the shoulder,
Can make one feel confident and bolder!

It's a silent and important way,
To tell another they're OKAY,
A simple touch upon the arm,
Is often loaded with caring and charm!

Let's stop and think for a little while,
A touch we could call a tactile smile,
Think about a handshake or hug,
It makes one's heart go chug, chug, chug!

Where am I going with a poem of this kind?
Think a moment, pretend you are blind,
A touch is really a tactile smile,
It will lift one's spirits for quite a while!

So if you know a person who's blind,
Keep this thought in your mind,
A tactile smile will mean so much,
In other words, a hand shake, hug, or touch!

How you use your wonderful voice,
That is simply your personal choice,
Sitting and standing straight and erect,
Will have on others, a positive effect.

Wearing a smile upon your face,
Will convey friendliness and grace,
A touch, a hug, a shake of the hand,
Says to another, "I think you're grand!"

Dear Reader: I'm going to allow myself to get personal for just a minute. I have just reread the poem above and I am sitting here emotionally TOUCHED in such a warm and positive way. It speaks to my heart. I enjoyed reading it again. I read it with my BrailleNote, reading one stanza at a time.

Some deep feelings and reflections were ignited within me. At the bagel shop just a few days ago my friend Nina and I were talking, drinking coffee, and munching on our bagels. Matt, a fitness expert and friend, happened to enter the shop. He came over and the three of us became engaged in an interesting discussion. Probably Matt was smiling as we talked—I'll have to ask Nina. Here's the enriching experience I had as we chatted. Matt, as he made a point or expressed a thought, would touch me gently and kindly on the shoulder. Please give that just a moment of thought. What do you think that meant to me? Yes, indeed, it meant friendship, acceptance, respect, etc. It was so important in terms of communication.

I wonder if tactile smiles are as significant to people who see as they are to me. Notice that I am not saying that tactile smiles have the same effect on others who cannot see, but I would conjecture that they do.

When I was in school in the 1940's, we learned about the five vowels. However, we did not spend any time playing with them, exploring words and talking about the importance of vowels. I think our vowels are really interesting and worth playing with and thinking about.

I can't resist inserting this riddle into my volume of poetry. Question: Can you find any word or words in the English language in which all five vowels appear in alphabetical order? I will include one word at the end of this chapter where this is the case.

Off we go to what I hope will be fun and thought provoking—my poem about vowels!

VOWELS

Twenty-six letters has our alphabet,
The vowels are considered a special set,
Our vowels give life to everything we utter,
Whether we speak clearly or whether we stutter!

About our vowels - there are just five,
Those five little letters keep our language alive,
Five important letters keep our language great,
They allow us words to communicate!

Those five vowels that I think are so great,
Let's take a moment to articulate,
They are letters one, five, nine, fifteen, and twenty-one,
Can you name them? go ahead have some fun!

What's with these numbers! How about a name!
After all, that's how they achieved their fame,
In order they are: A, E, I, O, and U,
Only five but they have lots to do!

Vowels form at least twenty-five percent a word,
That is, of every word I've ever heard,
Here's a challenge for you to take,
See if I have made a mistake.

Cake is fifty percent vowel,
Forty percent of the word towel.
Vowels are forty percent of the word chair,
Prove me wrong, if you dare!

Let's look at the word basement,
The three vowels are really the cement,
Thus, three letters out of eight,
Make the word basement, that's great!

Whoops! I'm really not all that bright,
I just discovered that I'm not right.
You can scratch what I just asserted,
I'm not right you should be alerted!

The word "scratch" makes me incorrect,
Count the letters and think of the effect.
The letter a is the only vowel,
This might make you laugh, it might make you howl!

So let me revise my observation,
I do this now without hesitation.
Every word that I ever knew,
Has at least one vowel; it is the glue!

These five letters, u, o, i, e, and a,
Are involved in every word we say.
Vowels are my friends; they are great,
They allow us to communicate!

A CONFESSION: I will not resist this desire to confess this to you. Shortly after writing this fun little poem I was standing outside my door waiting for my friend, Nina, to join me for an enjoyable fitness run. I was thinking of my assertion that every word was made of at least 25% vowels. All of a sudden I realized that I was incorrect. The word "scratch" popped into mind and, bingo! I discovered that I had made a mistake. Thus, I added this confession to the poem. Right here is one example of the fun of vowel-playing. I wish that back in my teaching days I had challenged my youngsters to play around with vowels. I might have made spelling easier and more fun. Now, moving on to my next poem about communication. I was stimulated to write this one by my granddaughter Emma and grandson Dave. They were eleven and eight at the time. We talked together about vowels and the consonant y, which is a part-time vowel. Enjoy!

MR. PART-TIME VOWEL

One letter in our alphabet is rather rare,
It's letter 25 and I hope that you care.
What a job it has, I do declare,
It works so hard, is that fair?

"The letter 'Y', of course," I heard you cry,
"The 25th letter is the letter Y!"
An exciting letter that is so, so busy,
Don't look too hard it will make you dizzy!

The letter "Y" has its claim to fame,
I think we call it a consonant by name.
As a consonant, YAAH is the sound that "Y" does say -
Examples are young, yes, your, and yea.
At times it's a vowel sounding like eee,

Examples are happy, many, and pretty.

And then, it may sound like the letter I,

In words like try, cry, and fry!

Yes, the consonant "Y" can be a vowel part-time,

For that there's really no reason nor rhyme.

For me this causes a little mystery,

I guess it's all a part of history!

The next poem deals with experiences that I have had over a rather lengthy period of time. You might say that it is sort of a pet peeve of mine. I wish that upon your reading of the poem we could sit together and exchange our thoughts and our experiences. Interestingly, I suspect that the people who do what I talk about in the poem are not even aware that what they say as they answer the phone sounds like gibberish. They probably unknowingly fall into the habit of answering in the manner that they do.

ANSWERING THE PHONE

Sometimes I call an office or store,

The person who answers is such a bore.

The tone of their voice is lifeless and drab,

They're not happy; they may be a crab!

Sometimes when I call a business place,

It sounds like the person is in a race,

They speak at such an exaggerated rate,

I don't understand a word they state!

If I owned a business, the person present
Would answer the phone sounding very pleasant.
The caller would feel a sense of gladness,
Not a sense of depression and sadness!

If I ran a business, whoever answered my phone
Would speak slowly, clearly, with a happy tone!
Each caller would be treated as welcome and such,
They'd know they were appreciated very much!

I don't know about you, but when people take time to remember my name and to use my name in a greeting or conversation it gives me a good feeling. I like to think that when I talk to others and use their name that it gives them a good feeling about themselves. In a sense, it says to them or to me that I am an individual. That I am unique—which we all are. Thus, I submit my next two poems for your reflection.

NAMES ARE IMPORTANT

A name is important to everyone,
To have no name would be really tough,
Life would be hard and not much fun,
Living without a name would be mighty rough.

To have no name would be so drab,
Of your name please be proud,
Without a name you might be a crab,
Tell people your name clear and loud!

Let me make this perfectly clear,

Your name is a noun to enjoy,

Speak it confidently year after year,

Whether you're a girl or a boy!

The following poem is an extension of the poem above. I think it may enhance communication between individuals. Just maybe, in a small but important way, by using a person's name you are recognizing them as unique and special. Perhaps I am exaggerating a little but nonetheless, anything we can do to treat people as one-of-a-kind seems a bit on the positive side to me. Let's see what you think!

ADDRESS PEOPLE BY NAME

In a store or on the street,

A friend or acquaintance should you meet,

That friend or acquaintance—how do you greet?

Saying hello is rather nice,

The two syllable word breaks the ice.

"Hello, hello." You could say it twice!

Well, you could say a simple "Hi,"

And simply pass each other by,

Or look the person in the eye!

Perhaps you would use a much better way,

Address them by name and make their day,

A person's name is important to say!

You have treated them rather specific.

Hopefully it will make them feel terrific.

To conclude this chapter on communication, here's what you've been waiting for: **the answer to my riddle**! Here is the challenge again, followed by the answer.

Challenge: Name a word in the English language in which the five vowels follow one another in alphabetical order.

Answer: The word is <u>facetious</u>!

An Afterthought:

In the process of putting together Chapter 8, "HUMOR OR RUMOR." I decided to explain how I organized my poems. They are organized, based on the type of poem, in folders on my Secure Digital Card. For example, the folder for the poems in this chapter is titled Communication; the poems that are in Chapter 4 are in a folder titled Self-Talk. In the Humor folder, as I was putting together Chapter 8 – HUMOR OR RUMOR, I discovered a poem that I named, "TELEPHONE MESSAGE." You may agree that it needed to be moved to the folder labeled Communication, and included in this chapter. To me this poem conveys an important message. It offers some advice to people who call and leave a voice message. Let's see what you think.

TELEPHONE MESSAGE

Some people leave their message too quick,

With those people I have a bone to pick,

When giving their number they do blast,

They spit it out—oh, so fast.

Ted Lennox

It's hardly possible for me to grab it,
These people should work to break that habit!
Say your number and do not mumble,
Don't talk so fast that the numbers jumble.

Speak your number nice and slow,
Speaking clearly is the way to go,
Each number you should articulate,
Slow, clear, and loud, would be just great!

CHAPTER

4

TAKE A WALK AND
TRY SELF-TALK

This chapter includes four poems dealing with the topic of SELF-TALK. I think this is such an important topic that I am devoting an entire chapter to it. For those of us working at improving each day, SELF-TALK becomes so important. What we say to ourselves is absolutely vital. What thoughts and feelings we program into our subconscious, into our amazing computer, determines the quality of our lives.

I believe that we all should listen to ourselves. We should be aware of our internal thinking; be aware of our programming. Then, we should alter any SELF-TALK that tells us anything negative about ourselves. We need to program into our subconscious minds ideas of being limitless; ideas that we are competent; notions in which we proclaim our abilities constantly.

Thanks to a man named Shad Helmstetter I got going with positive SELF-TALK. Because I am in the process of sharing much of my life with you through poetry, I want to say that until I read Shad's book about Self-talk, so much of my thinking, my programming, was that of negativity. I often doubted my abilities and my self-esteem was much too low. Shad's book about SELF-TALK got me into the wonderful adventure of reprogramming myself. Now I endeavor to DIE Daily— that is, Dream, Improve, Enjoy!

For those who might be interested, the name of Shad's book is:

<u>What To Say When You Talk To Yourself</u>
It was published in 1982 by Pocket Books,
a division of Simon and Schuster.

Shad writes seriously about the four levels of Self-Talk. The four poems in this chapter deal with each level. Perhaps you might be interested in what those four levels are before you get to them. They are: Level One, "I Can't", Level Two, "I Need To", Level Three, "I Can", Level Four, "I Am".

SELF-TALK
LEVEL ONE: I CAN'T

We talk to ourselves through the day and night,

What we say can frighten or delight.

From ourselves the messages we receive,

To an extent will determine what we achieve!

Observe, if you will, where your mind does dwell,

Your SELF-TALK can keep you in heaven or hell.

What you say to yourself can fill you with gladness,

Or it can load your heart and mind with sadness!

There are four levels of SELF-TALK we'll explore,

To life they can shut or open the door.
I CAN'T! is what we'll call Level One,
A lackluster life is all you'll have won!

"I can't do math," thinks Michelle,
To himself, Sam says, "I can not spell."
Then there's Pam who often proclaims,
"I CAN'T remember people's names!"

The second level of SELF-TALK on a behavior and thinking basis is about the same as the "I can't" level. It is the level where we acknowledge or recognize that we need to make a change. Shad Helmstetter labels this level the "I need to change, I ought to change, I should change." In other words, the individual recognizes the need to change and improve, but in reality makes no effort or decision to inaugurate SELF-TALK that would create a change to their life.

Putting the matter just a bit differently, the individual does not initiate a SELF-TALK plan that will lead to the desired change and altering of thought, feeling, and behavior. In other words, there is no change in the individual's SELF-TALK that would lead to reprogramming the subconscious and conscious mind.

In my case, I looked at my beliefs and my thoughts, and I consciously began to program into my mind words and thoughts that would change my perceptions and programming in the direction that I wanted to go. I abandoned the "I NEED TO" level of SELF-TALK and replaced it consciously with the SELF-TALK of level three and four.

SELF-TALK
LEVEL TWO: I NEED TO

The second level of SELF-TALK is called "I NEED TO,"
This level describes many people not just a few.
Another name for this level is "I wish I could,"
Or, alternatively, "I really should."

"I need to stop smoking," utters Bill,
"I want to get organized," mutters Jill,
"I wish I were more creative," stutters Phil,
"I should lose ten pounds" is the thought of Lil!

At this level of SELF-TALK is problem recognition,
To solve the problem there is no decision,
I need to change but I will not,
Is about as far as you have got!

The first level of SELF-TALK is "I can't."
The second level is "I should, but I shan't!"
At these levels we do not improve,
Let's use self-talk to make a positive move!

The next two levels are mighty important. They are the levels of SELF-TALK where we improve our lives and ourselves. The upcoming poem represents level three; it is the level of SELF-TALK in which one programs into their subconscious mind ideas and concepts that build improvement, confidence, and happiness. We are now talking about the level of SELF-TALK in which is programmed the idea "I no longer." Let's allow the level three SELF-TALK poem speak for itself.

I personally started programming level three and four into my subconscious on the night of May 1, 2003. I had been unhappy, my confidence was very low, and I was miserable and depressed. I will get to that a little later in this chapter.

Once again I started reading Shad's book, and I initiated my SELF-TALK program which I have been faithful to ever since.

SELF-TALK
LEVEL THREE: I CAN

Hold on! This level gets so exciting!
It's full of hope; it's truly delighting.
At this level your mind and heart begin to sizzle,
With this SELF-TALK you will not fizzle!

At level three you change your SELF-TALK,
Your programming is different as you sit and as you walk.
"I can," are the words that underscore this theme,
They allow you to believe, they allow you to dream!

"I no longer smoke," declares Harry,
"I do not swear anymore," states Mary,
"I no longer worry," are the words of Horace,
"I am well organized starting today," asserts Doris!

Let's say that smoking's a habit you'd like to break,
Starting now—a cigarette you will not take.
Oh wait! Let us think this project through,
First, something much more important you must do!

To yourself be very kind,

Let's reprogram your wonderful mind.

Programming your subconscious is the first step to take.

First a short program let us make!

"I don't smoke! I don't smoke!" please declare,

"I only breathe in healthy air.

I don't smoke, and I'm not sad,

In fact, inside I'm really glad!"

Tell yourself as you light a cigarette,

"I do not smoke and there's no regret."

Program "From cigarettes I am free,"

What you program in a short time will be!

Programming through SELF-TALK is a terrific route,

Shortly, those bad habits will be given the boot.

By using SELF-TALK you need only decree

And soon from smoking you will be free!

Write a script which says "I can." "I don't."

It will not be long before you won't.

Read that script twice per day—

Soon the habit will have gone away!

The fourth level of SELF-TALK is the "I AM" level. It is an important level because it helps you become what you want to be. At times we hear people say that they are trying to find themselves. The idea here is that they believe in themselves as a unique individual, and they want to get in touch with that uniqueness. And indeed we are all unique, and so in a sense the desire to find oneself has meaning. That is, we want to know ourselves and express our special and unique individuality. In fact, later on in the chapter entitled "REFLECT, RESPECT, CONNECT," there will be a poem that I have titled "WE ARE UNIQUE."

Perhaps instead of saying "I want to find myself," we might throw more light on the concept by stating "I shall or I am in the process of creating myself." Would you agree with me that a statement like "I am creating myself," puts us in charge of the direction we desire to take. That is, we are in charge of our own programming; we determine what we want to be. We create ourselves!

The question arises "If we have the wonderful and noble aim of creating ourselves, then how do we go about programming that into our subconscious minds?" I suggest that through SELF-TALK we can do just that. We can write and say SELF-TALK affirmations that will alter our conscious and subconscious thinking, allowing us once again, to CREATE OURSELVES. Jeepers! What a powerful and wonderful notion! In Shad's book he gives many guidelines for doing just what we are talking about.

The poem that follows is the fourth level of SELF-TALK. Shad calls it the "I AM" LEVEL. Here it is: Let's see what you think!

SELF-TALK
LEVEL FOUR: I AM

Just as levels one and two go together,
They'll both hold you back in any weather,
Levels three and four make a wonderful pair,
Into your life they'll bring fresh air!

In level four, of your life you are in charge,
You take control- you are the Sarge.
Or should I say you are the captain of your ship,
Your life becomes a glorious trip!

Your programming is all achievement bound,
Not a negative word can be found,
Tell yourself that you are able,
And my friend, that is no fable!

"I am really a wonderful guy,
And that's the truth, not a lie."
"I am truly a fabulous female,
My self-talk keeps me on the positive trail!"

Watch your SELF-TALK night and day,
Monitor it as you work and as you play.
Do positive programming without regard,
It is easy; it's not hard!

Fill your mind with positive belief,
Do not allow any negative relief!
Say to yourself words that lead to success,
With negative SELF-TALK do not mess!

"I AM good at running track,
Speed and endurance I do not lack."
"I CAN read and understand,
In school I'm really grand!"

Use SELF-TALK to move you along,

Go through life singing a confident song.

Level FOUR of SELF-TALK is your version,

It will make your life a great excursion!

Learn to say to yourself "I Will, I Can."

And now, when should this SELF-TALK for you "began"?

This very minute is the time to choose,

Why not? What in the world do you have to lose?

CHAPTER

5

I DON'T MIND BEING BLIND

Reflections About Not Being Able To See

In this chapter there are six poems. Some of them are serious; some of them are on the humorous side. Perhaps they will lead you to some interesting thinking.

Let me start by telling you that I have been blind all my life. Being blind in no way interrupts a person's having a successful, happy, and meaningful life. Each of us, and I do mean each of us as individuals should develop our abilities. We should be happy about the adventure of using our God-given talents, skills, and abilities. None of us should spend time dwelling on our inabilities, our lack of skills or talents. In other words, our minds, our programming, our SELF-TALK should be filled with positive thinking. However, you know that already if you have read the poems in Chapter 4.

So! Here's where I start with my first poem called, "TO BED WE GO." Please enjoy it. Following the poem, there is a neat little drawing of my wife and me in bed. There is a lamp beside her, and she is reading away. The braille version of this book will include tactile drawings of the same picture. Thus, a person who is blind will also have the pleasure of a tactile or touch picture to accompany the poem.

TO BED WE GO

At the end of the day and it's time to sleep,
Into the bed my wife and I creep.
Reading is a hobby which is her delight,
She flicks on the lamp and reads into the night!

Does it bother me or keep me awake?
Not at all; in just a few minutes sleep will overtake.
She reads and the light burns on so bright.
I've slipped into dreamland for a glorious night!

Does her light bother me, you may wonder.
No, I'm bothered more by lightning and thunder.
I sleep away, she reads along,
Together we sing a terrific song!

Sometimes at night sleep has her in its power.
It's then that I may read for up to an hour.
I read away as free as a dove,
Enjoying lying beside my love!

Ted Lennox

I read away without a concern,

For nary a light do I burn.

She sleeps away without fail.

Guess what! My reading is done in braille!

We both can read in bed at night.

My wife she needs to use the light.

As for me, I go from dot to dot.

As for light, I need it not!

About reading in bed we never fight,

We both can read well into the night.

She reads away with the light so bright.

I read away in the dark, that's right!

I hope that brought a smile to your face. I confess that it does to mine.

Since we are talking about braille, my next poem will be about braille. It will give you a glimpse into the beauty of the braille code, and into the fantastic importance of braille for one who cannot see. In fact, let me just state it this way. Braille is as important to me and to other people who are blind as print is to you. Take a moment, if you will, to think how important print and the ability to read are for you throughout the day. You will realize how fabulous braille is.

During my teaching career I had the privilege of being a guest instructor at Eastern Michigan University. I often taught a class labeled: "Introduction to the Exceptional Child." One of the assignments was to simulate a specific handicap and one of the choices was to be learning disabled for 24 hours. Those who chose that handicap could not read for a 24 hour period. What a challenge that was to my students! Many of them told me that they learned more in that 24 hour period than anything else they learned for the entire semester.

Along with this poem about braille please look at the drawing which features the six basic dots that make up the braille code, and the letters a, k, and u. As you read the poem look at a, k, and u, and discern the relationship that the poem articulates.

Braille Cell

Raise dot 1 and it is Letter A

Letter K

Letter B

Letter L

Letter C

Letter M

Letter D

Letter N

Letter E

Letter O

Letter F

Letter P

Letter Q

Letter G

BRAILLE IS BEAUTIFUL

I go through my day from dot to dot,

Braille is beautiful, I like it a lot.

These six little bumps have great appeal,

With my fingers I just have to feel,

And the world comes alive and the world is real.

Dot one alone represents a,

Add dot three and it becomes k.

Dots one and two are b I'll tell—

Add dot three and by golly it's l.

Dots one and four make the letter c,

To make an m just add dot three.

Dots one, four, and five gives you d,

Add dot three and n you'll see.

Dots one and five make the letter e,

To make an o just include dot three.

Feel dots one, two, and four, it's f you'll see—

Hey! Now annex a dot three, and bingo - - the letter p!

Letter q is one through five,

Delete dot three and g comes alive.

So! What do you think - - how are we doing thus far?

To the letter h add dot three to get an r.

It's easy; just dots two and four.

Plug in a three and you've got an s for sure.

T is simply dots two, three, four and five, and hey,

Guess what! Take away dot three, you'll have a j.

A to k and j to t,

Just jump ten letters and add dot three!

Now to your a and k view,

Annex dot six and there's a u.

To b and l attach dot six, let's see,

By George! You have made a v.

From c to m to x we jump,

Just by adding one little bump!

D to n can soon become y,

Just add dot six did I hear you cry!

Let's go from e to o, add dot six for the letter z.

Are we home? Are we done? Are we free?

Not free, but hang loose- we're almost done.

Thanks to Louis we're in for some fun!

The letter w creates some thought,

No w exists in French we're taught.

We'll create w by using our j,

Come on! Let's think- there must be a way!

Ah, yes! We can get out of this fix,

To the letter j just add dot six!

Yes, braille is beautiful I must say,

It opens life's doors in many-a-way!

The freedom it provides is many-fold,

It's better than silver; it's better than gold!

As in the previous poem the braille version of this book will include a tactile drawing comparable to the print drawing above.

While you are reading this poem using the printed word, pause for just a moment and think how important the printed word is for you. You read constantly: books, magazines, mail, ads, bills—maybe you'd like not to read those! When you do take a moment to reflect on the importance of reading, it will underscore the meaning in the poem.

The reference to the name Louis in the poem refers to good ole Louis Braille who invented braille in the early 1800's. He sure had a profound impact upon my life! My salubrious friend Nina has encouraged me to insert a bit of history about the development of braille. A fascinating captain named Charles Barbier, in Napoleon's Army, in the early 1800's, developed a means of reading in the dark. His system of communicating was done by touch and was based on a twelve dot configuration. The purpose of his touch reading system was so that Napoleon's soldiers could communicate with one another and not expose themselves to the enemy after dark. It was a great idea but too complex for the soldiers' fingers to utilize.

In 1823, Captain Barbier was invited to the school for the blind in Paris where he showed the faculty and students his invention. A young student named Louis Braille became interested and motivated. Louis was about 14 years old. He revised Barbier's system, making it a six-dot platform. Thus, the fingers could feel it more efficiently. The preceding poem explains the braille code as it was devised by Louis. So what started out to be an Army weapon has led to the enrichment and enhancement of many, many lives. This is a topic so meaningful to me that I'd like to pursue it much further, but this is basically a poetry book to let's move on!

I will admit that the next poem has important emotional meaning for me. The poem dismisses a myth that many, many people tend to believe. It has bothered me for years. Writing this poem has evaporated that sense of being bothered, and I do not get disturbed when people accuse me of living in a world of darkness. Off we go to the third poem in this chapter. Read, reflect and maybe revise your ruminations. Whatcha think?

WHO'S IN THE DARK?

Most people think that if you can't see,
In the dark you will always be.
They think that darkness is a constant state,
Morning or night, early or late!

Now if you will please listen to me,
Darkness and light are for those who can see.
Darkness is only for those who have sight,
Think about it and you'll know I am right!

In order to know dark you must know light,
Darkness and light are a visual flight.
You cannot have one without the other,
Think about that my sister and brother!

So! if you are blind, you do not know dark,
Whether at home or out in the park.
And if you are blind, you know not light,
Light is reserved for those who have sight.

Darkness exists not for those who are blind,
Light is not part of a blind person's mind!
To know visual experience you must have eyes,
As for the darkness myth, it's met its demise!

Now speaking for myself as one joyful guy,
I tell you the truth, I would not lie!
I've never been in the dark day or night,
Nor have I experienced what sighted people call light!

This is not sad, please believe me,
Just enjoy sight if you can see,
Just know that I do not live in the dark,
Whether at home or out in the park!!

My next poem, "COLORS ARE ONLY WORDS TO ME," introduces you to my daughter Amy. In 1978 she was just eight years old and had a Saturday morning paper route. One Saturday I was carrying the load of papers and she was running them up to the porches. It was in April and the grass was turning springtime green. She mentioned how green the grass was, and I off-handedly said, "Well, Amy, green means nothing to me." She stopped dead in her tracks and in utter astonishment she said something like, "Dad, that is amazing! You don't know what green is?"

Ted Lennox

So now, for the poem.

COLORS ARE ONLY WORDS TO ME

My wife says "blue is my shirt,"
She often says it is covered with dirt.
She tells me to change it and don't be hurt,
Sad to say, my response is often grouchy and curt!

I should be grateful for her kind concern,
There is a lesson here for me to learn.
All I need do is change my dirty shirt,
And then my wife with me will flirt!

This colorful world must be something! to see!
I chuckle 'cause it means nothing to me!
It enriches life for people with vision,
I long ago made that decision!

I encourage all of you with sight,
Relish this colorful world day and night.
Take time to enjoy each beautiful hue,
That's the positive thing to do!

As for me colors mean nothing at all,
The beautiful colors that come every fall,
The gorgeous green and flowers in spring,
To me none of these mean a thing!

My world is made of sound and touch,

For me these characteristics mean so much.

Am I sad because color is forsaken,

That this aspect of life from me has been taken?

Although it would be interesting to see the colors of Earth,

Its absence has never bothered me since birth.

I do not miss what I cannot know,

Internally, life has its exciting glow!

In order to live a life that is stable,

We all should emphasize of what we are able.

Upon your abilities focus and dwell,

You will find life exciting and swell!

So back to color for one more sec,

For me there only words, so what to heck,

For me colors are really not real,

My life is filled with texture and feel!

I just re-read the above poem and I admit that I have been somewhat misleading. I have overstated the truth. It is tempting to remove this poem from my book but instead let me amplify and clarify what I mean.

Within the poem I rather strongly indicate that to me color means nothing; colors are just words. What I mean to convey is different. First, color does mean a great deal to me. I love it when my friend Ali, who is a Michigan Wolverine fan comes up and teases me because I have on a blue shirt - - Michigan colors. I'm a Michigan State Spartan

- - color green! When Laura tells me that my shirt is blue and my pants are brown that means much to me. I thank her and go change my shirt! I love to hear that the roses are red, and that the trees in the fall are BEAUTIFUL.

Thus, the poem above is simply saying that, because I am unable to see, I do not personally understand purple, pink or polka dot. I hope, oh! I hope, you understand. It is SO important to me that I do not mislead you in any way.

I cannot resist adding another adorable and amiable Amy story. Three months later, in July, I took Amy and Marla to a church retreat. Unfortunately, Laura was unable to go. The retreat was held at a camp on a pleasant little country lake. It was Saturday afternoon and I was peacefully sitting on the beach socializing. Amy came to me and asked if she could go swimming. Of course I endorsed the idea happily. She asked if I'd go with her to the ladies' cabin while she put on her bathing suit. As we walked through the woods, I told her that I could not go in the cabin but would wait for her on the steps. She simply, matter-of-factly, said, "Dad, you can come in while I change. You wouldn't be able to see any ladies dressing or undressing." I will stop here and let you decide what I did.

Here is one more story that fills me with a joyful memory.

When my daughter Marla was twelve years old, Laura and I were to pick her up at school upon her return from a soccer game. We got there at the appointed hour, and no Marla. As we waited I became worried. Finally, I said to Amy, let's go inside for I think I need to inform the police just as a matter of safety. I dialed 324-4405 and the policeman at the desk answered. I explained our situation. He then asked, "What is your daughter's name?" Then, "What color is her hair?" Amy was in the hall, so I yelled, "Amy, what color is Marla's hair?" The policeman abruptly hung up.

You might be interested in my next move. I called Richard Wagner, our mayor, and told him what I had done. He said, "I'll get a policeman right over there." Amazingly, and happily, within a minute or two, two vehicles showed up. One was a police car, the other wonderfully delivered my darling daughter. My precious family still teases me about that – 29 years later.

Thank you, dear reader, for reading this and allowing me the joy of a superb memory.

The next poem which I gently call, "IN THE RESTROOM," is I hope a bit amusing. However, it is absolutely true. Take time to look around the next five restrooms you visit and note how the various items can be almost anywhere. I never know when entering where anything is located. OOKEEDOOKEE- read, enjoy, and reflect!

IN THE RESTROOM

As you read this please keep in mind,
I am writing this because I am blind.
I hope I don't make it too confusing,
Although it is true, it's meant to be amusing!

There are bathrooms large and small,
In homes, restaurants, and shopping malls.
They are necessary for one and all,
Blind or sighted, short or tall!

Ted Lennox

Once I pass through the bathroom door,
I'm confronted with a whole new world to explore!
One thing I don't have to find is the light,
I leave the light for those with sight!

Now if I have to go real bad,
When I find the toilet I am glad.
The toilet paper is hidden I think,
Left, right, high, low, under the sink!

It's time now to wash my hands,
Finding the water handle makes its demands.
Some bathrooms have their own way,
Just stick your hands out and there's the spray!

Sometimes you just have to turn the knob,
When discovered that's not a bad job.
Some handles you only have to twist,
Easy enough once you get the gist!

But wait! Where to heck is the soap?
I will find it; I do have hope!
It could be high, it could be low,
Where it is you never know!

We've washed our hands and emptied our bowels,
But where, oh where! Are the paper towels?
To left, to right, in front behind,
What did the architect have in mind?

Each bathroom keeps you on your toes,

Where things are located one never knows.

Just go ahead with a spirit of joy,

Whether you're a girl or whether you're a boy!

COLOR REVISITED

Now let's take on color from a different point of view,

The words we'll talk about have nothing to do with hue.

Ironically, you can't see them even if you can see,

These colors lurk inside both you and me!

Ted Lennox

You meet a friend and say:
"My friend, how do you do?"
He says, "Here's how I feel today!
I'm really feeling rather blue!"
In this case blue has no visual appeal,
It is referring to something you feel.
Visually the color blue is normally nice,
The feeling blue is a sad device!

Now let's look at the term called red,
Visually it's cheery and bright, but instead,
Red referring to a feeling denotes not glad,
It says that you are REALLY mad!

He gave me a push and I'm seeing red,
I'm feeling angry with him is what I've said.
The color red is bright and cheery,
The feeling of red means you're mad and dreary!

Is there such a thing as a little white lie?
Do lies vary in degree from small to high?
That's something upon which we can reflect,
Or should the truth always be given respect?

At times people tell a lie that is white,
The word white has nothing to do with sight.
It only tells us what kind of lie,
Has been told by some girl or guy!

So people enjoy a sweater that's blue,

But they don't enjoy feeling that way 'tis true.

We enjoy so much wearing red,

The color red is truly a treat,

But, red inside can lead to defeat.

If lies can be white, can they also be pink?

Tell me now, what do you think?

When color refers to something you do or feel,

You don't have to see it and yet it is real.

When this poem is over and through,

I'll still laugh when I think the BLIND can feel BLUE!

In 2002 an innocent and enjoyable telephone call led to my introduction to this fantastic BrailleNote. The lady who told me about it is named Collette. Collette is one of those people who are so straight forward and hopelessly honest. For thirty years she has been telling me that she is five feet eight, 124 pounds, with gorgeous red hair! (:-) WARNING: Were you to meet Collette you might not recognize her even though I have given you an accurate and vivid description!

When she told me about this new gadget, the BrailleNote, I discovered that our Special Education Department just received one. So thanks to Collette this opened up a whole new way of conducting my life and my students' lives. Enough said. The following poem will give you insight into the power of the BrailleNote. Please read with understanding.

Ted Lennox

THE BRAILLENOTE

I love my BrailleNote,
Upon it I dote.
It has my vote,
It's better than a car, better than a boat!

What does it do, you may ask.
It will help with many a task.
It's a computer and it does so much,
It speaks to the ear and it speaks to the touch!

It will output information straight in braille,
With my fingers I read without fail,
It also will speak to me, I do declare!
Sound waves come to me right through the air!

Speech or braille I may choose,
There's no way that I can lose.
But listen to this I want you to know,
Braille and speech together can flow!

So I can use speech or I can use braille,
But both together can be used without fail.
Braille or speech, speech or braille,
Or use them together, how can I fail?

I can write a note, document, or letter,
How could my life be any better?
To the internet I can meander,
I can go to any web site and have a gander!

I can google to my heart's content,

There's no web site to which I cannot went.

A google map I can get in braille,

Laura and I travel and we do not fail!

This book is written on my BrailleNote,

The spelling checker I used as I wrote.

The dictionary I use continually,

My vocabulary has improved fabulously!

The BrailleNote also has a calculator,

For doing figures what could be greater?

From simple to complex you are free,

You can even deal with geometry.

E-mail you can send, receive and save,

About the e-mail program I really do rave.

For the first time in my life I can read e-mail,

It's available in speech or in braille.

There are many other things that I do,

Perhaps I might mention just a few.

There's games and music I do declare,

I just download them right through the air!

There is a program that's called Keyplan,

It's great for any lady or man.

My dates and alarms it will keep,

Keeping me on schedule or wake me from sleep!

Ted Lennox

About my BrailleNote I really do rave,

I think I'll take it with me to the grave.

It helps me to live a wonderful life,

There's only one thing better and that's my wife!

CHAPTER

6

REFLECTING, RESPECTING, AND CONNECTING

In 1999, my friend Jesse, also my son-in-law, e-mailed me a message which I found fascinating and significant. The concept in the message was that we have 86,400 seconds each day. My thought was "Why not use those seconds to live fully?" It eventually lead me to write this poem entitled, you guessed it, 86,400. Perhaps you, too, will find the idea fascinating and meaningful. And for the fun of it, take time to do the math and see if my figures are accurate. Thanks, Jesse!

I just reread the poem and upon completing stanza one I threw up my hands, I smiled broadly, I laughed aloud, and I'm laughing right now as I write this to you. If you will, read stanza one and then take time to reflect upon the humor intended. I am tickled, and I hope you will be too!

Ted Lennox

86,400

What in the world could this number be for?
I hope it's not someone's golfing score!
Or let's hope it's not how much I weigh,
For golf I would not be able to play!

Let us think in the direction of time.
Hopefully you'll find much reason and rhyme.
In the math that I will express,
So off we go! We will not digress!

There are 24 hours in every day,
In which we can work, sleep and play,
We can dream, and think, and cogitate,
Let's try to make each hour great!

In every hour 60 minutes are given,
Let's make each minute a moment for livin',
There are 1440 minutes per day,
Let's take each minute to swing and sway!

I'm sure you know that we're not yet done,
There's one more step and it's kind of fun.
Get ready to use your lively mind,
This will be exciting, I'm sure you'll find!

60 seconds in every minute—you bet!
60 times 1440 and what do we get?
Why not stop right here and calculate,
A five digit number will be your fate!

86,400 seconds per day,
A truly exciting figure I'd say.
You can count them—it's up to you,
As for me I've got other things to do!

Let's give each second our very best,
If we do, our life will surely be blessed,
Each second is a gift from Heaven above,
Fill it with life! Fill it with love!

We have 24 hours every day,
1440 minutes you say,
86,400 seconds hurray!
Let's go out—live and not delay!

The following poem means much to me. In it I open up my heart to you and you will be introduced to a very important part of me. I want to share with you my feelings, and one of my passions. After reading this poem I hope you will feel that you know me better. I truly do love poetry.

Ted Lennox

WHY I LOVE POETRY

I like to read poetry,
It does something special for me.
In just a few words one can state
Thoughts that are funny, thoughts that are great!
Poetry can state thoughts that are profound,
Amusing thoughts also can be found.
There's a feel of joy, a moment of bliss,
A poem is akin to a caring kiss!

Poetry is similar to a song,
You can say so much without being long.
A boost to the spirit, a shot in the arm,
Poetry is loaded with loads of charm!

In just a few words you can say so much,
Through a poem a life you may touch.
A person can feel down in the dumps,
Reading the right poem may bring joy, even goose bumps!

For me poetry is really a balm,
It's very much like a beautiful psalm!
I love my poetry collection,
There's value in each and every selection!

Each day I read a poem aloud,
It boosts my spirit; it makes me proud.
Music and poetry is good for the heart,
It's a terrific way for a day to start.

The third poem in this chapter is called, "BOOMERANG." My awesome grandson Dave, at age nine, had talked about living in Australia when he grew up. My fellow teacher and dear friend Bonnie went to Australia one summer and I asked her if she'd bring me back a boomerang. She did! So, one of Dave's presents that Christmas was a boomerang.

It struck me that words are in some ways like a boomerang. The words we send forth into the world are often like boomerangs. Kindly words return to us kindness. Unkind and hostile words often come back with unkindness and hostility. Thus, I Wrote the "BOOMERANG" poem. So thanks, Dave.

BOOMERANG

If you want your boomerang to return,
You first must throw it into the air.
This is an important thing to learn,
So throw your boomerang if you dare!

Here's a thought, we all need to know it!
So grab your boomerang let it fly,
To get it back you must first throw it,
It has to sail out into the sky!

Let's take this thought in another direction—
Our words are boomerangs that we throw.
Boomerangs and words—is there a connection?
Like boomerangs words will return to haunt us or help us grow!

It is important how we use our voice,
Send forth words of kindness none other,
The words we use are our personal choice,
They'll be good for you and good for your brother!

Verbal boomerangs we throw into the air.
Choose your boomerangs with kindness and care.
Verbal boomerangs should be filled with respect,
For your words with others you do connect!

DECIDE TO LIVE

Once you decide to live,
Your heart and soul to life you'll give.
You won't look back,
You'll look ahead,
You'll live each moment until you're dead.

Happiness will be in every thought,
Contrary to the way we often are taught.
You'll know nothing but positive emotion,
For life you'll feel nothing but deep devotion.

In the title the first word is decide.
That word is important I wish to confide.
Deciding is an essential skill,
We should decide or our environment will!
Learn to decide and enjoy the thrill!

Having decided, now you can start

Living your life straight from the heart.

Each thought, each feeling, filled with sunshine,

On each moment you surely will dine!

My next poem is simply called "DETOXIFY." Here detoxify means to rid yourself of poison. The purpose of the poem is that of dumping (detoxifying) destructive thinking especially destructive thinking patterns. Many of the poems in this chapter deal with the notion of trashing destructive thoughts and replacing them with dynamic and positive thoughts.

The poem came about because of my dear friend and running partner, Nina. She attended a Detoxification Seminar and shared with me the many detoxification affirmations which they learned. Off we go!

DETOXIFY

Toxic is a word that can give us thought,

Poison is a synonym I have been taught.

Let's apply that word to how we exist,

Just a suggestion but I wish I could insist!

I might say to myself today

My house I shall detoxify right away.

A strange use of the word I will confess,

But it fits—my house is really a mess!

Detoxify yourself with proper nutrition,
That would be a very good decision,
Keeping toxins out of your blood,
Keeps it clear and not filled with mud.

Here's where I'm going with this important verse
TOXIC thoughts: What I ask, could be worse?
I encourage us all to detoxify our brain.
Detoxification—what an awesome refrain!

Now am I talking about a proper diet?
Yes, but more, don't tell me to be quiet,
Let's go in another direction as we detoxify.
Listen to my plea, listen to my cry!

Our minds, our brains, let's diffuse,
Erase those thoughts that only abuse,
They keep us from living our life with zip.
Detoxify your brain, life will be a glorious trip!

We detoxify our home making it neat,
Our blood we've cleaned from head to feet,
Think a moment and maybe you'll find,
To take time each day to detoxify your mind!

To detoxify the brain—what does that mean?
It sounds so wonderful, in that direction I lean,
It's all about the thoughts that we embrace,
Do they handcuff us or take us to open space?

If we are to detoxify our brain,

What do we mean by this beautiful refrain?

To detoxify the blood, the muscle, the cell,

Eat properly, and that will keep us well!

You can toxify or detoxify your mind,

Are your words, your thoughts, harmful or kind?

Do you think, "I'm having fun."

Or, do you think, "I wish this day were done!"

Do you think, "In this moment I rejoice!"

Or do you think with a sad tone of voice?

Say to yourself, "My life is divine!

I'm full of joy! Everything is fine."

I could go on and on with these detoxifying notions,

For happiness and joy they are such great potions.

Just detoxify your mind continually,

You will be happy, and you will be free!

The next poem, to me, has an interesting title. It is called "ENCOURAGE OR NAG." It has many applications. It can apply to husbands and wives; it is an important element in friendship; and it surely is highly relevant when it comes to mothers and fathers relating to their children. From my viewpoint, encouragement is such a powerful part of any relationship. Yet, especially in close relationships like the three mentioned above—marriage, parent-child, and friendships, it is so easy to focus on the negative and to <u>harp</u> at or <u>nag</u> people. My motto is ENCOURAGE, ENCOURAGE, ENCOURAGE. Please be alerted just because that is my motto does not mean that I always follow it. Just ask my wife, children, and friends!!!

ENCOURAGE OR NAG

With our friends and with our spouses,
We can be heroes or we can be louses.
About them we are free to praise and brag,
Or we can choose to be a miserable nag!

If you want your marriage to be loaded with life,
Take time each day to encourage your husband or wife.
Your friends, they too, you might motivate,
They will think of you as really great!

However, if your spouse and friends you do nag,
They will probably look upon you as a hag.
Don't badger them with a barrage of words,
They will only think that you're for the birds!

So if your tongue you like to wag,
Don't use it as a tool to nag.
Encourage, encourage, let me plead,
Do not nag no matter the need!

To friends and spouses give positive support.
As to nagging, please do not resort.
Do what you can to help others to achieve,
Encouragement is important I do believe!

Oh! my goodness, I just had a thought!!

Here's something I wish I had been taught!

Encourage children, encourage adults,

You're sure to get terrific results!

One more thought I'd like to share,

Show yourself how much you care.

Encourage that friend who's always there,

He-she's with you 24-7!

Encourage yourself and get closer to heaven!

In November of 2004 I had the privilege of being in Roscommon, Michigan. I was there to teach a seminar on the use of the BrailleNote. The BrailleNote is a wonderful and powerful computer which allows me to get and produce information in braille, speech, or both. Dominic Gagliano, a rep for the company that manufactures the BrailleNote, loaned me a small and special version of the BrailleNote, which they named PK, for the evening. Fascinated with it, I took it to bed, played with it and wrote the following poem, "THE END OF WAR."

Now here's why I tell this little saga. Several weeks afterward I realized that I wanted that poem for a calendar I planned to give my wife Laura for her birthday and the poem was on the PK I had returned to Dominic. I contacted him, and with much joy I discovered it was still there and Dominic kindly took the time to e-mail it to me.

In the following poem the precise history probably is not completely correct. However, it is close enough for me. I would just like to mention that when World War II ended I was twelve years old. I truly believed that there would be no more war on this marvelous earth of ours, and that we'd live with each other in peace forever.

This now is my goal, my hope, my dream, and my prayer.

END OF WAR

1945 ended the war.
We all thought there'd be war no more.
From sea to sea and shore to shore,
We knew for sure there'd be no more war!

We'd live forever with peace galore,
1945 brought peace to earth forever more.
August of that year we thought gave birth
To peace and love hereafter on Earth!

What should happen five years later-
There was fighting in another world theater.
Korea north and south was the spot,
Fighting there was deadly and hot!

Many soldiers lost their lives,
Never to come home to their husbands and wives.
We finally were able to quit the fight,
Thanks to a guy whose name was Dwight.

In the sixties came Vietnam,
More shooting, killing, and many a bomb.
People were killed left and right.
Isn't war a terrible fright?

Eight bloody years on foreign soil,

Think of the land, lakes, and lives mankind did spoil!

This happened in 1975,

From Vietnam we finally did flee.

For sixteen years it was great,

Then off we went to Kuwait.

More lives we humans did spoil

Because of the underground gold called oil.

That war, thank God, was rather short,

Now we had oil by the gallon or quart!

No more war in the Middle East,

Sadam's hands were tied! Oh! What a beast!

And then there came a terrible shock!

We found ourselves invading Iraq!

When will war end, I cannot say,

Let's hope and pray we'll find a way!

It would be a victory oh so great,

If we all could learn to tolerate.

We all could live with laughter and mirth,

If only we'd commit to peace on earth!

I'm turning my attention to the important topic of motivation. This poem talks about our motivating others and about others motivating us which leads me to think about and encourage and motivate myself. All three notions are valuable and so helpful; that is, it is good to motivate others and have others motivate us. We should all keep that in mind. However, INTERNAL, or SELF-MOTIVATION is a characteristic for which we should strive. At least that seems highly significant to me. Read the poem and please decide what you think.

INTERNAL MOTIVATION

It is nice if you, me motivate,

If I motivate you that's great!

Let's motivate each other each moment of the day,

Support and encourage each other all the way!

To motivate others is a wonderful trait,

It fosters love and certainly not hate.

When it comes to motivation from others,

Let's not depend upon friends, sisters or brothers.

It's internal motivation for which we should strive,

That will keep us passionately focused and alive!

Our thoughts and feelings should make us rich,

They'll keep us on the highway, not in the ditch.

Think thoughts and feel feelings that motivate,

You'll help yourself to make your life great!

Motivate yourself and it's full speed ahead,

Motivate yourself from now 'til you're dead!

Positive motivation is what we should chase,

It will fill one's life with meaning and grace!

MY BEST FRIEND

We each should have a very best friend,
Someone who'll stick with you from beginning to end,
Someone who'll support you and help you mend.
I believe I am setting a brand new trend.

I used to think my best friend was my wife,
She's been that for me most of my life.
She supports me through victory and through strife,
A fabulous friend is my wife!

There are other friends who are so, so dear,
They are always with me through joy and fear,
They provide for me a glorious mirror,
They help me my ever exciting life to steer!

My friendships help keep me on track,
They keep me looking forward not back.
With friends like mine, riches I don't lack,
They make my life simply mirack!

Ted is the friend who likes me best,
He helps me fill my life with zest.
He's present always in play and rest,
It pleases me to get this off my chest!

Whether I'm alone or in a crowd,
He always tells me of me he's proud.
His words to me I'm happy to receive,
For in myself he's taught me to believe!

Ted Lennox

My friend Ted is a great motivator,
He is not the kind of guy who is a berater.
His words to me are always upbeat,
Being with him is always a treat!

He helps me to live a lively life,
He loves himself; he loves his wife!
Ted tells me to love myself without regard,
Then, loving others is never hard!

If you don't love yourself, oh brother!
You simply cannot love another.
Start loving yourself and you will find
To others it's a pleasure to always be kind!

This is truly great advice,
Very likely I'll read it once or twice.
I'll need to work to achieve it,
To this project I must commit!

Now Ted, I think we need to have a talk,
Keep this concept in mind as you walk.
Don't just read it and set it aside,
Keep it in mind through the day as you stride!

This poem talks about attributes that I wish I had had all through my life.
I must confess that that has not been the case. As part of my fascinating

life, for the past few years I have worked to achieve these wonderful characteristics. The attributes I am addressing are: *KINDNESS, CONFIDENCE, ENJOYMENT, DREAMING, IMPROVING, and PEACE.* For me, and I speak only for myself, these six characteristics enrich one's life dramatically. Along with math, reading, and history, I wish my parents and teachers had taught me these marvelous traits.

So, with this in mind and the acronym KCEDIP, here is my poem!

MY PLEDGE TODAY

Be Kind

Let me keep this pledge in mind,
Today to myself I shall be kind!
Kindness to myself is where I must start,
This kindness should come from deep in my heart!

If to myself I will be loving and kind,
Then what do you think that I surely will find?
So kindly I'll be to my sisters and brothers,
Kindness will be an easy expression with others!

Be Confident

In order to function as I should,
To myself I must be good.
I must be confident with my every thought,
This is wisdom that I should be taught!

Ted Lennox

Confidence is a great attribute,

To a wholesome life it's truly the route.

I must be confident with my every feeling.

When it comes to confidence, there's no wheeling, no dealing!

Enjoy

Each moment of life I shall enjoy,

I hope that's true for every girl and boy!

Enjoying life I hope you'll agree,

Is a vital goal for both you and me!

No matter what I'm doing right now,

Whether mopping the floor or milking a cow,

Whether I'm laughing and chock full of glee,

Or in the bathroom taking a pee.

Every moment I'm filled with life,

Whether shining my shoes, or hugging my wife!

I want to live in a joyful calm,

This is my code, this is my psalm.

Each moment of life I seek to enjoy,

My life is such a wonderful toy!

Dreams

Here's a thought and here's a scheme,

Each day I'll take time to reflect and dream.

We all should dream both young and old,

Dreams are truly more precious than silver and gold!

Of this we all can be so proud,

Spend time each day with your head in a cloud.

Dreams are so important to life for each,

This is something school really could teach!

Improve

Let us stay and live in this groove,

To work each day to improve.

Improving each day is what I savor,

I want my being to express that flavor.

Improving, improving, hour by hour,

That gives life a wonderful power!

Peace

Abiding within our heart, mind, and soul,

Living in peace is a wonderful goal.

Each morning we might sign a daily lease,

To live each moment in comfort and peace.

Peace allows us to use our resources,

To control our minds and harness our horses.

Peace frees us from outside forces,

We are in charge of all our courses.

I'm sitting by myself in the living room. It is 2:09 AM. I just read the previous poem out loud to myself. It boosts and inspires me. One element for me in terms of poems and poetry is that I find it meaningful and valuable to read aloud. Somehow hearing myself read it just adds a highly enriching aspect. If you haven't already done it, maybe, just maybe, you might wish to try the enjoyment of reading poetry aloud.

Let me just humbly say thanks to you for reading this poem.

How in the world might I convey to you, my happy reader, how I feel and think about the next poem? It is called, "PEACE ON EARTH." Peace on Earth would be so wonderful. We all could live such joyous and peaceful lives. It seems to me so obvious and so simple. Yet thus far we have not taken all the gifts we have here on Earth and put them to good use all the time. Yes, indeed, we do use them for good, for happiness, and so forth, but then we also use them to hurt one another. You will see what I mean right now as you read the following poem. May I say that this comes from my heart to yours, perhaps.

PEACE ON EARTH

Human beings have such fabulous potential,
To use that potential I think is essential.
Why don't we keep peace one with the other,
We are all in a sense sister and brother!

We have come so far as the human race.
We had no understanding of our earthly place,
We wandered about as nomads do,
Rummaging for food and water too!

We invented the "wonderful" valuable wheel,
The wheel has been a significant big deal.
We learned to plant crops and settle down,
People settled in homes, villages, and towns!

Because we made us of the magnificent wheel,
It eventually led us to the automobile.
We no longer sleep on the ground or in a tent,
We build houses made of wood and cement!

Thanks to Wilbur and Orville Wright,
We now can fly both day and night!
We have radio, TV, and electronic phones—
It's simply fantastic how humans have grown!

We all can write, we all can read,
And consider the importance of math indeed.
Just think somebody somewhere invented the zero,
Whoever it was I think they're a hero!

Then, there's the role of electricity,
It deserves a lot of publicity,
For the little electron we all should care,
Constantly filling our lives with flair!

I could rave on and on about the human race,
And how much good we've achieved on our earthly place.
Now with satellites we have cyber space.
With computers life takes on a while new dimension,
We've arrived at new levels of comprehension.

Ted Lennox

So, let's look at the other side of the coin,
For a moment my thoughts please join.
What I'm about to say is very forlorn,
It breeds not joy but rather scorn!
When people lived in the style of a nomad,
They often treated one another so sad!
The bow and arrow was a blessing you say,
And I agree with you all the way.

But often arrows were used to hurt one another,
They were used to damage both sister and brother.

People drive automobiles even when they are drunk,
What in heavens name could they have thunk?
War airplanes have been used to destroy
Many-a-girl and many-a-boy!

Just think a moment about nine eleven,
That's close to hell—certainly not heaven!
In World War II bombs were dropped on England and France,
Those humans chose to kill rather than dance!

Everything we have can be used for good or bad,
Why some people choose to go with the bad—how sad.
Can't we all just share our Earth?
Starting right with the day of our birth!

Let's use each item we have on loan—
Computers, cars, and telephones,
Use them to promote both peace and love,
Until off we go to new life above!

If we ALL lived in peace while we're here
There'd be plenty of food, clothing, shelter, and cheer,
Everyone could have an abundant life,
Full of joy and free from strife!

Let's, each of us, use our marvelous mind
To be at peace and always be kind.
If ALL would be a sizzling success,
The world would not be in such a mess!

Go forth today and peace declare,
Send only joy and goodness into the air.
Let's use everything on this marvelous Earth
For peace, for joy, for kindness and mirth!

Use nothing, that's nothing, in a negative way,
Keep everything positive day by day!
Everything that you and I think and do,
Should be used for peace, is that not true!

I had the good fortune of working almost seven years with my friends
Ralph and Del. It was Ralph and Del who launched my adult life. We

taught together as a team from the time I was 23 to the time I was 30. I know not what would have happened to me without them. Ralph and Del were friends, parents, coaches, you name it—they were that. I could spend many pages talking about them but they are mentioned here because they used to laugh good naturedly and tease me pleasantly about my habit of procrastinating.

I never told them, because I did not realize until years later, that I procrastinated out of fear, anxiety, and worry. I was fearful of doing certain emotional things, so it was normal for me to procrastinate. I will admit that a big item on my IMPROVEMENT list even now is that of overcoming procrastination. I'm very serious about this. It is my desire that you find this poem interesting and that you understand the perspective from which it has been written—mine! Please understand my use of the notion "procrastinate procrastinating."

PROCRASTINATING

I wonder what makes me procrastinate.

It's a habit that's not really great,

It gets in the way of not getting things done,

Procrastinating is really not very much fun!

Many times when I procrastinate

It's because of fear, and that makes me late.

Overcoming fear is a positive trait,

Then you can live at a more peaceful rate!

Here's a notion I am contemplating,

I could procrastinate not procrastinating,

If I keep procrastinating as a daily style,

I can procrastinate not procrastinating for a while!

Did I really write that paragraph?

If so, in a way it's making me laugh,

Thinking deeper, it gives me a lift,

Procrastinating not procrastinating takes quite a gift!

There is a saying that goes around,

To follow it is not too sound,

"Don't do today what you can do tomorrow"

Basically leads to frustration and sorrow!

The bottom line is to do things today,

To procrastinate is not the way,

So off I go to get things done.

And along the way I'll take time for fun!

The two upcoming rhyming adventures are an important piece of advice to the guy writing this volume. They are called "SEIZE THE MOMENT" and "SURVIVE." During my lifetime I have failed so much of the time to heed the advice in the following two poems. Instead of seizing the moment I'd fret and fuss about things, I'd worry, I'd be fearful. I'd be seriously concerned about what others were thinking of my words and my actions. Now that I've started I could go on and on about my worries and doubts and fears, but I will go to the next two poems and read them aloud. As stated earlier, I find that reading aloud has value. It will keep my attention and not let my mind wander.

It is 5:15 AM and in one hour it is off to the track for a 5-mile run and talk with my friend Nina. I'll start my day with the advice from the following poem in mind and I will make every effort to put it into practice.

SEIZE THE MOMENT

I talk not of hocus pocus,
On each moment we should focus,
To each moment give your full attention,
Later on you'll have full retention!

Focus on peace all the time,
Make each moment really sublime,
Add excitement to this equation
And you'll find joy in every occasion!

Focus your heart, body, and mind,
And I am sure that you will find
You'll be happy all the time,
Your life will be so sublime!

If you do you'll be astounded,
Your whole being will be totally grounded,
Life will be a glorious breeze,
So each MOMENT let us SEIZE!

SURVIVING

Yes, it is important to survive

But that's not the meaning of being alive.

When we are alive then each moment we should thrive.

Hello life, "gimme five"!

I plan and pray that I have drive,

I'll make the most of being alive,

Not to merely exist and survive!

On this earth I want to thrive.

So! Here's the goal for which I'll strive—

To live each moment with joy and jive,

At this goal I'll strive to arrive,

I'll aim higher than to merely survive!

The next poem contains 532 words. It is titled, "SYMPHONIC LIVING." Basically it is a metaphor comparing a symphony orchestra to an individual. That is, an orchestra has several sections. There are percussions, wind instruments, brass, string instruments and so forth. When an orchestra plays together in harmony it is beautiful. We humans might think of ourselves as having different sections, that is, thoughts, feelings, attitudes, and such. When we have all our parts or sections playing in harmony, we too can play a beautiful rhapsody.

Toward the end of this poem I consider the conductor of our orchestra. I propose that each of us should conduct our own orchestra. In other words, our internal world should be in harmony—our thoughts, feelings, and our behavior. That harmony should be beautiful and wonderful. Further, the proposition is that we should be the conductor of our orchestra and not be controlled by outside forces—that is, by others or by circumstances.

Having stated this as a little essay, let's get to the poem. What do you think about this poem?

SYMPHONIC LIVING

An orchestra makes a beautiful sound,
The music reaches your heart and soul,
If well played nothing sour can be found,
That is the purpose- that is the goal!

All the instruments need to blend,
A symphony should produce joy and beauty,
A harmonious message they should send,
That is their aim and in a sense their duty!

There should be no sound that's cacophonic,
Now there's a word I rarely use,
Each melody should be oh so symphonic!
So cacophonic's a good word to choose!

The tuba should not just blast,
The violin should not play off key,
the clarinet should not play too fast,
The trumpet should not resemble a buzzing bee!

Each section should fit into the discussion!

The string section must stay in sync,

So should the instruments known as the percussions,

Tell me now what do you think?

Each orchestra has a conductor,

The conductor's job is to orchestrate,

The conductor is the orchestra's instructor,

Keeping all instruments in harmony is simply GREAT!

Where am I going with this rhyme?

I hope to talk with you from my heart.

For me what follows is rather sublime,

So I am going to give it a start!

Our lives should be like an orchestra playing,

Inside we should experience happy harmony.

A sonorous life we should not be betraying,

So let's eliminate all the cacophony.

One section of our orchestra is instruments we call emotion,

We need to allow emotion to play life's tune.

Joy, happiness and love should be the promotion,

Anger, hate, depression, we should eliminate from June to June!

Our personal orchestra has a section called thought,

Our thoughts should radiate beautiful sound.

Confidence, kindness, limitless we all should be taught,

Not a discordant thought should be found!

Ted Lennox

Our attitudes are also part of our being,
Play your attitudes with a harmonious jive,
From all harmful attitudes we should be fleeing,
Your personal orchestra will come alive!

Our behavior should be a sweet melody,
With all our instruments inside and out,
Expressing a beautiful rhapsody,
Playing notes of hope not notes of doubt!

The parts of our orchestra are stated thus,
Thought, attitude, behavior, and emotion.
If played in harmony, what a plus,
We'll be able to live with such joy and devotion!

Does my orchestra have a conductor you might ask?
If so, who is that conductor, please tell,
For my conductor has an important task,
My conductor needs to do his job well!

Each of us our own orchestra we should direct,
We all should be in control day in and day out.
Our music should have a beautiful effect,
Peace, joy and harmony should be our route,

So, my friend, do for yourself this wonderful favor,
Conduct your orchestra to play peace and caring.
A beautiful life you will savor,
Each section should flow in symphonic sharing!

Conduct your orchestra yourself, my friend,

Each part of your orchestra just smoothly blend.

Let your life play a beautiful song,

Play it each day all day long!

Play your symphony from dawn to dawn,

Let your orchestra express its potential,

Play it from birth until you're gone,

That is important, that is essential!

It is early Wednesday morning about 5:00 AM. As I took my last sip of coffee, I thought, "What should I write to introduce this poem called, "TONIGHT?" You will recall that this book starts with the poem that I use to launch my day. Well, my first thought was that perhaps I should use this poem as I retire for the night. In fact, that was why I wrote it a couple of years ago. But, guess what, I think I've only read it maybe twice or three times since. I am wondering if perhaps I should read the poem each night to end my day. That could lead to reflecting about the day and evaluating it in terms of the poem I use to kick off each day. I'll think about that, but it does sound like a rather fair idea. I'll try it tonight!

OK my friend and my reader, thanks for listening and allowing me to share who I am. By the time you're through this book you'll know me rather well. Thanks again for your interest.

I just copied the poem onto the BrailleNote clipboard, switched to this chapter and pasted it. When I read it again I knew I wanted to provide you with a short explanation which is important to me.

The poem is only eight lines long, but you will find 12 lines. How do I say this without getting into a lengthy dissertation? I think of each of you as unique, truly special, and important; i.e., I did not want to address just boys or just girls. Maybe I should add another stanza proclaiming that, first and foremost, You are You, <u>then</u>, you are a girl or you are a boy. Whether you are a girl or a boy, be happy about that and proud of that. OK, Ted, take this advice and move to the next poem.

TONIGHT

As I put myself to bed this night,
I say to myself clearly and loud,
This day has been a total delight,
Of my thoughts I am certainly proud!

It is true I am one happy boy!
This whole day has been loaded with joy.
Each moment I've lived with zest and zeal,
My life is rich, my life is real!

It is true I am one happy girl!
This whole day has been a joyful whirl,
Each moment I have lived with zest and zeal!
My life is rich, my life is real!

I genuinely wish that I had known and understood this concept as a boy and as a young man. I have spent much too much time trying to be what I thought others thought I should be or wanted me to be. I failed to understand and to develop and to be proud of my unique being. What a joy it is to allow yourself to be yourself; to work smilingly at creating yourself. The old saying from Shakespeare "To thine own self be true" comes to mind. When pondered over, if taken seriously, this thought can be most enriching.

Having said these things about each of us and our wonderful uniqueness let's take a gander at the next poem, "WE ARE UNIQUE."

WE ARE UNIQUE

Truly, truly, I know this is true,

There is no one exactly like you!

We need to know that we all are unique,

Unique from the top of our heads to the bottom of our feet!

Physically, it is obvious to us all,

Some of us are short, some of us tall.

To describe each of our bodies would be all right,

But that is not what I have in my sight.

I do not want to ignore the physical part,

From inside out including your heart,

Your eyes, your ears, your tummy and toes,

Your shoulders, your arms, your legs and your nose,

We are all physically unique,

We should appreciate one another from head to feet!

Inside our bodies we are all so rare,

Knowing ourselves is an adventure, a dare.

We are made of so many miraculous parts,

Our thoughts, feelings, and experiences give us a start!

Ted Lennox

First and foremost think of yourself as a treasure,

Being yourself should be a glorious pleasure.

Comparing yourself to others should become but a fable!

Live your life and do what you're able.

Observe, study yourself and reflect,

Always give yourself much respect.

Value yourself and enjoy who you are,

Traveling your own highway will take you far!

Your mind differs from Sue, Jack, and Tim,

Your feelings are not exactly like her or him.

We are all part of this great universe,

Each of us different, unique, and diverse!

So take time yourself to know,

Enjoy the thrill and bask in the glow.

Enjoy your uniqueness as you go,

Be mindful to enjoy all the unique people you know!

All right, now that we have established our awesome uniqueness let's take the next step on the road to living a full, happy, and satisfying life on this marvelous earth. Here comes a plea to be ALL that we can be. The key words in the next poem are: limitless, set no limits, and unlimited. These, of course, are synonyms.

This, my friend, will probably be the final poem in this chapter unless of course I should write another before this book is completed. It may be of interest to you as it is to me to note that these poems appear in alphabetical order. (In a moment of caution I just checked the above statement and discovered that I was wrong. The poems are almost in alphabetical order. The second poem is out of place.) If my granddaughter, Emma, age nine, were writing this she'd probably put them in reverse alphabetical order.

A few months ago I was the speaker at Emma's Brownie troop in Morral, Ohio. Brooksie, one of Emma's friends, sang me a most delightful song. We all know the song about the ABC's that children learn. Well, and I am smiling big as I write this, Brooksie sang it backwards. It was great! Since humor is a part of this book, let me insert a funny joke the Brownies told me. Try this one—

Question: What do Elves learn in school?

Not to make it easy for you, the answer is at the end of this chapter.

SET NO LIMITS

I have something so important to say,
This message especially I want to convey.
At birth we are all given a brain,
It is crucial for us to train our brain!
Many people influence our mind,
Often unknowingly they are unkind.
We allow a fence around our mind to erect,
That fence- it has a powerful effect!

Too often a seed in us they plant,
That seed is known as "I can't."
Limits we place on ourselves: that's sadly,
Is there anything that could be that's more badly?

Ted Lennox

Think of our mind as a garden growing,
Each day it could stand a little hoeing.
Let's clear out every single weed,
Fertilize it with positive thoughts, indeed!

Let me state my case real plain-
We are taught to place limits on our brain.
We're not good at math, music, or art,
We learn these beliefs almost from the start!

Now here's another way to train your brain,
You are limitless is my refrain.
Please, my friend, do not limits set,
Limitless you are, you can bet!

How do you teach yourself this wonderful notion?
This should be a lifelong devotion.
Program yourself to believe this thought,
Over-ride every negative belief you've been taught!

There are techniques I'd like to share
Because for me and for you, I care.
This is a poem and I hope you'll keep reading,
Considering my thoughts and sincere pleading.

Let me suggest just one simple technique,
Maybe to your heart it just may speak.
Three times each day I'd like to suggest,
I think I too will follow this request.

Here we go with this Powerful thought,

"I am unlimited," despite what I've been taught.

That's just nine words every twenty four hours,

Do it for a month and enjoy your new powers!

Teach yourself about your unlimited brain.

I hope I don't bore you with this repeated refrain.

"I am unlimited,"- this thought you need to believe,

Then off you go to live and achieve!

ANSWER to the question: "What do elves learn in school?"

The Elfabet!!!

It is 4:00 AM and perhaps I should end this chapter and go on to Chapter 7. However, I am feeling so good but also sentimental that I want to share some thoughts and feelings with each of you, one-to-one, that are personal and private. I've not shared them with anyone before; at least not in this manner.

Here's what I'm feeling! I wish I could go back to high school, back to Sexton High in Lansing, MI. How much more I would have been engaged - in school, in classes, with friends and such. Then off to college. Although I really had my heart into my four GLORIOUS years at Michigan State, I wish I had believed more in myself and therefore made more of those wonderful years. For example, and now I do get personal, I wish that my thoughts had been different when I was on the wrestling team. When we were wrestling Indiana, e.g., as I walked on to the mat and shook hands with my nice opponent my thoughts were basically these, "I won't win." "Sam is a much better wrestler than I." "I know I will lose, but I hope I don't get pinned." (Fortunately I never got pinned.) My friend, these were the kind of thoughts that filled my inner world—my mind, my beliefs. In a way, no, in reality, the match was over before it began. Only I knew these thoughts.

I should have shaken hands with Sam, wished him well, and then my thought should have been something like this: "I can win this match." "I will wrestle and have fun, and I certainly plan to win." "I am a good and capable wrestler." These thoughts never entered my mind. My thoughts were all negative, all about knowing that I would be defeated.

Thanks for taking time to read this. The bottom line is that all that is over and it is my business and challenge and joy to live fully each day of the remainder of my life.

Here's a P.S. I have been away from this chapter for a while. But I return from Chapter 8 to include my poem about coffee. I decided that it would be best included here. It is not humorous; it is more reflective than anything else. It just tells you how I start most of my days. I like to launch my days in a positive way, as you know!

COFFEE

My coffee is a wake-me-up!
I start each day with a freshly brewed cup.
I sit in my chair and sip away,
Thinking about how I will live this new day!

I lift my cup up to my lip,
Then I take a pleasant sip.
I sip, I think, I meditate.
Starting the day like this is great!

Many times I've heard people say that they want to find themselves. The following poem is in the same vein, but it suggests a little different approach. The poem suggests that perhaps we should be about the business, the exciting business, of creating ourselves. This is different than finding oneself. So here's the poem for your reflection.

CREATE YOURSELF

Many people have in their mind,
That it's themselves they are trying to find.
Who they are is hidden under a cover,
The challenge for them is one's self to discover.

To discover yourself let me not berate,
To know who you are is a worthy trait.
Here's a thought I'd like to suggest,
There's another route that might be best!

Ourselves we all should be working to create,
Whether early in life or whether late.
Creating oneself is a glorious mission,
Every child, from their parents, should have that permission!

To myself I shall send this plea,
I hope, self, you will agree.
Creating myself is a glorious task,
No better challenge of myself could I ask!

I will enjoy creating myself each day,

I'll start right now, I shall not delay,

I shall create myself from inside out,

My life will improve—there's not a doubt!

As I said earlier, I had a very brief career as a teacher, retiring after a short 47.6 years. I was so fortunate! My students were just fabulous and the people who were my colleagues were also my friends. I loved each day working with all of them.

My wonderful colleague and friend Margaret worked with me day in and day out for 27 years. In fact, in 1974 she was my student teacher. One of the many jokes that Margaret, my wife Laura, and I used to make went like this- I would introduce Margaret as my day-time wife and Laura as my night-time wife. Margaret used to quip, "And don't get us mixed up."

Here's one more quote. Margaret used to say that you could not spend a day in our classrooms without having several joyous laughs. That is totally accurate. Having given you this background let me share this pleasant poem with you.

HARD AT WORK

I told myself a little fib,

"I've worked hard all my life."

That's a statement that's rather glib,

My life's been fun not loaded with strife!

I'll think again and wisely discard,

The one word I must erase.

I'll scratch the adjective HARD,

"I've worked all my life," is now in place!

What I'm saying is that my work was rewarding and fun—

I taught kids who were lively and curious.

The day was over almost before it had begun,

We all enjoyed learning and were never too serious!

Seems like I didn't work hard each day,

Now I ask myself this simple question—

Did I work or did I play?

If you should have a suggestion,

Please send me that thought-wave this very day!

I guess I didn't work hard each day.

Here is the best that I can suggest,

Every day I was hard at play,

To be hard at play was my daily quest!

My students and colleagues were all sublime!

At work we all had a wonderful time!

The phrase "hard at work" could also be,

"Hard at play", by Jiminy.

Maybe I didn't tell myself a fib.

If I think of "worked hard" as really great,

That surely would not make me glib,

"Hard at work" now's a positive state!

Ted Lennox

In November of 2003 I met with our superintendent Randy Kite and told him that I planned to retire the following June. I asked permission to talk at the next school board meeting. I wanted to let the board members know publicly what a terrific career I had in Lincoln Park. Moreover, I wanted to tell them what an outstanding and super group of people I had worked with throughout the years.

When Randy and I finished talking in his office, he suggested that we might go to the board meeting room and he could show me around. He wondered if that would be something that I would like and provide me with a sense of comfort. That was a touching moment and a touching time for me. I had such a good feeling about our exploring the board room. Please realize that for me to explore a room is quite different from many of you who would just walk into a room, scan it with your eyes, and that's it. Randy and I explored the room through walking, talking, and touching. It was so meaningful.

The following May I got a call from the Central Office asking me if I really was planning on retiring. I, in surprise, said "Why yes." Then they informed me that I had to put it in writing in order to make it official. Here we go! I want to share my retirement letter with all of you because it underscores the previous poem, "HARD AT WORK."

RETIREMENT NOTIFICATION

May 11, 2004

I guess it's time for me to leave,

I can't help it if I grieve.

I'm now in my 48th year,

I think it okay to shed a tear!

My days in Lincoln Park have been packed with joy,

I'm indeed a fortunate boy.

My colleagues-"Wow!" What can I say?

They've been terrific in every way!

My former students, they live, work and pay

Their taxes each and every day.

Their heads should be held high in every crowd,

Of each of them we can all be proud!

So I submit this grateful letter,

My job here could not have been better.

At 11:59 on the 30th of June,

I'll jump up and commence singing a different tune!

You might say that I shall retire,

The truth is that I shall only rewire.

And this, my heart needs to convey,

May God bless you all in every way!

In the book <u>The Four Agreements</u> by Don Miguel Ruiz, one of those agreements is "Don't Make Assumptions." Perhaps I might mention that the book is talking about four agreements you make with yourself in terms of living effectively. Here is one example, hopefully meaningful, of the harmonious living one can achieve through not making assumptions.

Ted Lennox

MAKING ASSUMPTIONS

Making assumptions can really be fun.
We assume that tomorrow we'll see the sun.
We make assumptions both day and night,
Most of the time we are probably right!

There's one area of our assumptions we should drop,
Assuming what others are thinking and feeling we should stop.
We cannot know what's in another's mind,
Just remaining neutral is best you will find!

Your friend Sally passes you on the street,
With nary a word does she even greet.
She doesn't even give you the time of day,
She walks right by and looks the other way!

You assume that she's really mad at you,
So Sally, in the future, you will surely eschew!
You assume that she is mean, nasty, or unkind,
Maybe a better friend you should seek to find!

Why not think, "Sally did not speak as I went by,
That makes me curious and I wonder why."
Maybe Sally's mind is some other place,
It's very possible she didn't even see my face.

In the restaurant, there sat Frank,

He didn't speak—what a crank!

Maybe his thoughts were on a letter he had to write,

He was engrossed in what to say upon getting home that night.

I've called her twice without a reply,

"I assume she doesn't like me," is your sigh,

Later you find that she was really sick,

You jumped to a conclusion much too quick!

Assuming what others think and feel

Is living in a world that is not real.

Here's a happier, healthier way to live –

Avoid assumptions that are not affirmative.

CHAPTER

7

LET'S NOW DELVE
INTO THE TWELVE

In this chatty little chapter you will meet the twelve months of the year. Hopefully it will be fun, interesting, and spirit building. I enjoyed writing these little poems and just thinking about each month. Just as a matter of interest let me mention that the calendar as we know it started in 1582. It is called the Gregorian Calendar because in some way or other it started when a fellow whose name was Gregory was the Pope. Thus, the name Gregorian Calendar. In a fascinating way I will mention that before 1582, January first started on what we now call April first. Some say the idea of April Fool's Day started when January first was moved to its present date.

I believe that I will be able to resist adding comments before each month, so unless I change my mind the next twelve poems will follow one another without commentary—if I can resist.

JANUARY

We start a new year for it's January.
Are we excited or is it scary?
Will we make this year a year of delight,
Or will we exist in a mood of fright?

Forward we go with adventurous hearts,
Ready each morning for the day to start!
Let's live, let's love, and each moment enjoy,
Whether you are a girl, or whether you are a boy!

FEBRUARY

February is here- we're on the run,
Playing in the snow is lots of fun.
At the North Pole there could be a ton,
In Australia there's lots of sun.

Twenty-eight days is all we get,
It's our shortest month but let's not fret.
Twenty-eight days is a lot of time,
So make each moment rich and sublime!

Up out of his hole pops the little ground hog,
He sits their quietly on a log.
If he sees his shadow, he then will definitely get
Back in his hole, there are six weeks of winter yet!

Ted Lennox

Next on the calendar is something fine,
It's time to send a Valentine,
We express friendship to each girl and boy,
To let them know they bring us joy!

I used to teach, and after lunch
We'd celebrate with Sweetheart Punch.
Everyone brought liquid for the punch-
What they'd bring I had no hunch!

Every year was a different flavor,
The taste was always exciting to savor.
The color they tell me was always mellow,
It could be red, brown, green or yellow!

We each added our little share,
A token that said we really care.
We set aside reading and math
To spend a brief time on the friendship path!

A way back in 1732,
George Washington was born- 'tis true.
Presidents' Day is really a hoot,
Because we can throw in Abe Lincoln to boot!

As I said back in January,
This month can be exciting or scary.
Let's sally forth in February,
Making this month joyful and merry!

I thought I had covered February quite well,

Now on March one I still have something important to tell.

On February 27, 1920, we dropped a sad hypocrisy-

Finally, women became part of our democracy!

Will you stick with me for another verse?

It gets better and does not get worse!

Every fourth year it's exciting to say

In February, we get an extra day,

Not twenty-eight days but twenty-nine,

It's called Leap Year and that's just fine.

MARCH

The weather in March can change, you know.

One day we get plenty of ice and snow,

A day later here come the rays,

It's lovely and warm in so many ways!

There's a saying about month number three,

The saying's been around for a century-

It comes in like a lion and goes out like a lamb,

We could say it goes out so tame but comes in with a wham!

In March on Sunday number two,

We change our day and nighttime too.

At 2:00 AM our clock springs ahead,

Shoot! We lose a whole hour in bed!

Also in March we alter our day and night,

It's darker in the morning, at night there's more light.

Interestingly, when we do change our time,

There's more time to play, on ice cream we spend many-a-dime!

A personal thought I'd like to include,

Please don't think I'm being rude.

Light and dark mean nothing to me,

It only matters for those who can see!

Go forth, enjoy Daylight Savings Time,

Your evening time has really become prime.

For me, light and dark are only words,

I know it's light when I hear the birds!

On the Ides of March Julius Caesar was killed.

The king's position in Rome now had to be filled.

Julius was killed by Brutus- his dear friend,

King Caesar came to a horrible end!

Let's move on to something positive and exciting,

The vernal equinox is what I'm reciting.

Around the twentieth, on our equator,

Equal light and dark- what could be greater?

On the equator shines twelve hours of light,

On the equator there are twelve hours of night!

This is true for every place on Earth,

For one day- equal dark and light has a short birth!

So far this year we've had a ninety day gift,

Has each day given you a magnificent lift?

Or, have you just managed somehow to drift?

Now to April we shall shift!

APRIL

April has some sayings that are neat.

Let's note a couple with April we greet.

The snow is gone, the grass has riz,

I wonder where the flowers is!

And we are told about April's powers

In the saying: "April showers bring May flowers."

"Take me out to the ball game" is a song,

Sing it in April and you can't go wrong!

Yes, in April we begin the baseball season;

April's exciting and baseball's the reason!

Now in April some think there's something to dread,

That being that Uncle Sam must be fed.

On April 15 our taxes are due,

This is upsetting to quite a few!

For me, paying taxes is money well spent-

I sort of think of it as paying my rent.

What I ask and what I plead

Is that our tax money be used wisely, indeed!

1912, April 14, there was a terrible clunk,

The result being that the Titanic was sunk.

Into an iceberg it did smash,

It was simply a terrible crash!

About fifteen hundred people died,

I wish that you could say I've lied.

It was sad and it still is,

So let's think about when those flowers will riz!

April's the very first month of each year

That has just thirty days to appear.

In January and March there were 31,

February has 28 and then it is done.

At the end of April, 119 days have been spent,

Oh my! Oh my! Where has all this time went?

MAY

On May 5 back in eighteen-sixty-two,

Something important happened 'tis true, 'tis true!

The Mexican army defeated the French,

From the French their freedom they did then wrench!

Now from north to south, even in Ohio,

Many people celebrate Cinco de Mayo!

In North America live three great nations,

Cinco de Mayo is a great celebration!

Mexico, Canada, the USA,

Three great countries I must say.

Each of them has an independence day,

We all live in a democratic way!

Next comes something BIG! Oh, my brother!

This day is set aside for your mother,

It's always on the second Sunday in May,

It's known to all as Mother's Day!

So pay honor to the mothers in our land,

They are wonderful; they are grand.

Each mother deserves a special bouquet,

It's so good to celebrate Mother's day!

On the fourth Monday in the month of May,

We celebrate Memorial Day.

We take time to remember those who've passed away,

Many people think, many people pray!

May is a month when we pay respect,

May is a month when we do reflect.

In May the days are thirty-one,

Go forth each day and have some fun!

Ted Lennox

JUNE

Here we are- it's the month of June.

For we who like school, it's come too soon.

Many families go on summer vacation,

Cars are traveling all over our nation!

The third Sunday in June we celebrate

By letting fathers know they are great.

Thus we take time to honor our dads,

Honor is expressed by both lasses and lads!

Now, in the northern hemisphere,

Something happens that fills us with cheer.

We experience the longest day of the year,

In a sense our summer at last is here!

We welcome summer with a phrase so nice,

It is called the "summer sol-stice."

On June 21 or 22 we have the longest day of the year,

That's because the sun is so near!

In the north we are close to the sun,

A good day for picnicing and having fun.

There is lots of light and little dark,

Lots of time for golf or playing in the park!

Here is something of interest to ponder,

In Australia, which is way down yonder,

In June they have the winter sol-stice,

Their continent is covered with snow and ice!

We mow our lawns in the month of June,
In Australia they sing a different tune-
They grab their shovels and away they go,
Cleaning their cars and shoveling snow!

So far this year 181 days have past.
Jeepers! This year is going so fast.
In your heart sing a happy tune,
As you find joy in the month of June!

JULY

Welcome to the month of July,
It's on the fourth that our flags do fly.
Throughout the land fireworks light the sky,
We celebrate freedom and that is no lie!

It was not July 5, nor July 3,
It was July 4 that we became free.
In 1776 the Declaration of Independence our forefathers did sign,
From the English Empire we did resign!

Why did they name this month July?
It was named after a famous Roman guy.
Julius Caesar was the king of Rome,
And now two thousand fifty three years later he gets in my poem!

Ted Lennox

Okay, here's something interesting about July—
It may make you smile, certainly not sigh.
It's the seventh month in the year, and HEY!
There are seven months that claim a thirty first day.

Let's sally forth in this month of July,
Eat plenty of ice cream and maybe some pie,
And in each day, all thirty-one,
Be sure to include a little fun!

AUGUST

Let's see, what's happened in this month that's hot?
I think you'll find, quite a lot.
Here's an event about which I think you'll care,
It's the birth of a girl named Virginia Dare!

Virginia was the first English child born in the USA,
Somewhere on the east coast I would say.
August of 1587 was the year,
So she is the first child to grow up here!

August 14, 1935, Social Security came alive,
Which allowed lots of older people to survive.
Then, on August 26, 1920, whoopee!
The 20th Amendment set our ladies free!

Here's an important democratic truth,

Starting that day women could go into the voting booth.

One hundred thirty one years in our country's life

Before voting was allowed for both husband and wife!

In 1959 the last state joined our group.

We added something super to our fifty state soup.

Hawaii is the name of the state,

It's a state that's really, really great!

Other things happened in August that are exciting.

Right now inside me is a spark that is igniting.

Democracy took another forward jump,

More people got over the democratic hump!

Signed into law was the Americans with Disabilities Act,

It opened up life for many and that is a fact.

The ADA is the acronym,

It gives many people plenty of vim!

The Americans with Disabilities Act

Then became a legitimate fact.

Against another group there is no discrimination.

To me this law is simply a sensation!

August is full of awesome events,

People on vacation living in tents,

Almost time to get ready for school,

The month of August is surely a jewel!

I believe that I said at the very beginning of this chapter that I would make no remarks, but rather just have the poems follow one another page by page. Are you surprised that I now am not about to follow what I said, or are you surprised that I managed to get all the way to September before interrupting my months' poems?

I simply could not resist. As I read, "SEPTEMBER" poem, several stanzas made me laugh joyfully. Please take time to read the stanzas and enjoy them. Then, maybe share them with someone in elementary school. I think they'd find it funny; I hope they will and you will, too.

Now I shall get to the poem.

SEPTEMBER

In September we are at month number nine,

We'll start hearing such words as the scrimmage line.

The game of football will become dominant,

Terms like touchdown and field goal will be prominent!

For those between ages 3 and 21,

It's off to school and lots of fun.

Reading and writing and arithmetic

Makes us sharp, makes us quick!

In third or fourth grade we learn each times table,

9 times 6 is 55, that shows us that we are able!

We learn that kame is spelled with a k,

By golly, if so, in third grade we may have to stay!

Whoever is writing this poem should be in school,

Their spelling and math is that of a fool.

Check out your spelling and your math.

Dear Writer, you're surely on the wrong path!

On September 21, 22, or 23, no later,

The fall equinox comes north of the equator.

Equinox means equal day and night,

That sort of fills one with great delight!

Let's not forget our friends south of the equator,

They welcome spring, what could be greater!

Twelve hours of sun, twelve hours of dark,

This earth of ours is really a lark!

This September, have yourself a ball,

Welcome in a wonderful fall!

South of the equator say "Hi!" to spring,

Go out and have yourself a fling!

OCTOBER

In 1492 Columbus sailed the ocean blue.

Starting in first grade this is a rhyme that all of us knew.

He ran smack dab right into our land,

I think that that was rather grand!

Ted Lennox

On the last day of October, there's Halloween,
A more frightening day we've never seen.
Kids dress up like a goblin or a ghost,
They want to see who can scare you the most!

Out they go to trick-or-treat,
Spooky costumes from head to feet.
Their goal is that of getting plenty of candy,
So buy those treats and keep them handy!

On October first, 1908,
Henry Ford did something great!
The Model T- it was born,
I hope the horses did not feel forlorn!

The way we move from place to place
Took on a totally different face.
The Model T filled an important need,
From here to there we now could speed!

So, enjoy the cool and the beauty,
That's your choice but not your duty.
October's days number 31,
Plan each day to have some fun!

NOVEMBER

The days are shorter, the nights are longer,
Winter is coming and getting stronger.
There are four months that end in "ber",
Those four months- do you know what they were?

Our ninth month, it is September,
It has thirty days, do you remember?
Then we get our second "ber",
Yep! You're right, it's called Oc-to-ber.

Now here we are right in November,
To finish the year we'll jump to December.
One hundred twenty-two days at year's end,
Are all "ber" days, what a trend!

On the eleventh day we celebrate
Vets-men and women who are really great.
They protect our country day and night,
It's just too bad that we humans fight!

On the fourth Thursday we all feel perky,
We give thanks and eat lots of turkey.
The day is called the day of Thanksgiving,
It is set aside for loving and living!

So go forward today with joy in your heart,

Begin each day with a happy jump start.

Fill your mind with exuberant joy,

This is my wish for each girl and boy!

DARLING DECEMBER

Darling, dandy, delightful December,

Filled with memories always to remember.

Memories that really warm the heart,

Preparing us all for the New Year to start!

December 7, the attack on Pearl Harbor, such an outrage!

From history I wish we could erase that page!

Why can't we human beings learn to live in peace?

Why can't fighting from this day forth forever cease?

About the 21st we reach an interesting mark,

We have less daylight and lots of dark.

There's little sun, but lots of moon,

That doesn't make many of us swoon!

About fifteen hours of dark each day,

That means only nine hours of light, you say.

Some people suffer from that kind of spread,

They're filled with depression and a little dread!

We learn that on December 25 Jesus was born.

With Christmas in December, few can be forlorn.

So, deck your halls with boughs of holly,

With Christmas in December we all can be jolly.

End the year on a joyous note,

Into the New Year we all should float.

Having had 365 glorious days,

Let's end our year with joy and praise!

CHAPTER

8

HUMOR OR RUMOR

As I start this chapter I am not completely sure about which of my poems I will include. Maybe I should go through my poems and decide ahead of time but somehow I'm wanting to get started right now.

And you know what? Because by now you have stuck with me this far I am going to be completely honest with you. As I am commencing to write, I am starting to feel deep emotion and probably will shed a few tears. It is tempting to ask you to forgive me for telling you about this part of my life, but that's not right. What I want to say to you is thank you for your understanding and interest.

Here we go, my friend. Last Saturday, May 10, my fantastic wife Laura and I had a fabulous day. Our hearts were playing the same song. Saturday night we went to bed happily with love in our hearts. Sunday morning, Mother's Day, I was up early and brewed some coffee in our motel room. Incidentally, I often served her coffee in bed and that's because we loved each other and I wanted to do that. She used to want to reciprocate, but I don't like drinking in bed. Anyway, one of our jokes used to be that husbands should serve their wives coffee in bed and Laura would say, "Why, it even says so in the Bible." You might ask her, "Where does it say such a thing?" She'd say, smiling all the while, "Why, there's a whole book in the Bible about that." You might reply with surprise, "What book is that?" Again, smiling as I am now, she'd respond, "It's called he-brews!!!"

Now, where was I? I was bringing her a cup of coffee. As I patted her and gently shook her, I got no response at all. I raced across the room to the phone, dialed 911, then went back to her and tried to find a pulse. There was none. The bottom line is that my friend, my wife, my love of 45 years, 6 months, 20 days, and 17 hours had died in her sleep.

I could go on and on with this, but I'd like to get to my next poem. However, first, and I do mean this, you and I may not know one another but thank you for reading this with caring and understanding.

The first two poems in this chapter will be my golf poems. My brothers Frank and Cecil, when we were boys, included me in everything, especially our passion for playing golf. Just recently, we spent a wonderful week together playing Monopoly, Hearts, and reliving our boyhood together. We spent plenty of time on the golf course. The next poem is dedicated to them and to my incredible ability as a golfer!! In fact, please look just below the title to see who wrote this poem!!! If you find it hard to believe what I've written, please don't ask Frank or Cecil!

FOUR

By "Tiger Ted"

On hole number one I made a par,
That made me feel like a golfing star.
On hole number two it was a birdie,
About my golf game there's nothing dirty!
An eagle I made on hole number three,
It filled me with joy, it filled me with glee.
After three holes I'm three under par-
Let's hope the next six holes I will not mar!

Ted Lennox

Another eagle I did achieve,
I'm a great golfer you must believe!
On to five and another par,
On my score card it's like a scar!
Hole number six is five hundred eight yard,
I tell myself "this won't be hard."
Would you believe an eagle I got?
As a golfer, now I'm really hot!

Off we go to seven, eight and nine,
Right now I'm feeling oh so fine!
On seven I get a par minus one,
This golf game is really such fun!

Now off I go to hole number eight.
Today my driving, chipping, and putting is great!
Against me Tiger would not stand a chance,
Into the pros I surely should advance!

On eight, it's a drive, a chip, and a putt,
My golf game today is in the right rut!
Another birdie to add to my score,
This game of golf I really adore!
On hole number nine I hit my drive,
My ball is flying, it's almost alive.
I chip the ball- it's heading toward the pin,
Believe it or not, it just dropped in!

Hurray, hurrah! I scored twenty-seven.

This game of golf is like being in heaven!

Four eagles, three birdies, two pars,

I guess I'm one of those golfing stars!

Am I honest you may ask?

As I read this poem I do nothing but bask.

You can decide whether I'm honest or lie,

For me it's back to the golf course for another try!

PLAYING GOLF

I practice golf at the driving range,

To another golfer that's not a bit strange.

To all of you I'll make this confession,

I enjoy each and every practice session!

To the course I go for eighteen or nine,

My mind is happy, my heart is fine.

I concentrate on every swing,

Hoping my ball will really zing!

Often I hit a wonderful shot,

I think to myself, "Ted, you are hot!"

The joy I feel down deep inside,

From my friends I don't want to hide!

Ted Lennox

There are times that I hook or slice,

It's tempting to use words that are not nice!

Or if a putt should go astray

I try to control the words I say!

One of my joys is getting a par,

Although I'm not, I think I'm a star.

A birdie I haven't experienced yet,

But one day I will, you can bet!

I always take time to enjoy the weather,

With my friends it's good to be together.

The game of golf I do choose,

You always win, you never lose!

When golfing, each shot should have our full attention,

The preceding shots we should not mention.

This of yourself you should demand,

Focus your thoughts on the shot at hand!

In the winter of 2008 I got together with my brothers Frank and Cec. We joined Frank at his house in Keystone Heights, Florida. Our purpose was to enjoy one another as we did when we were boys. One day Frank and I, along with our wives Laura and Rena, spent a day at St. Augustine. The following poem will tell you what occurred.

YOUNG AGAIN

It's Poncé De Leon I want to thank,

This is true, I'm not a crank.

He landed where St. Augustine does now exist,

The year was 1513 according to the calendar on my wrist!

He looked and he found the Fountain of Youth.

Again, remember, I tell nothing but truth.

He'd be here today if he hadn't been hit

By an arrow that took his life and his wit!

In 2008 it was my brother Frank,

For this trip I surely must thank.

To St. Augustine he took me for a bit of history,

What happened there is quite a mystery!

We paid a visit to the Fountain of Youth.

Again, please know that I tell the truth.

A man named Kicking Wolf gave me a drink,

What happened then, take a guess- what do you think?

Before the drink I looked age seventy-four,

After the drink subtract fifty or more.

Now just look what happened to me,

I look twenty-four or twenty-three!

It is my hope and my plea that I won't offend you. In fact, there is a part of me that in a sense says, no Ted no, don't mess with our marvelous language and spelling. Then, there is another part of me that smiles, even chuckles, as I read this poem. I say to myself, "Why, oh why, should we be taking the time in school to teach kids that you must spell rong- wrong? Why not just spell words like they sound?" Spelling would then be so easy or should I say eezy.

As I reread this poem I could not help but chuckle with amusement. So please read, enjoy, reflect, and agree or disagree, or have mixed feelings like me. If you choose, send an email with your thoughts or opinions. I will find pleasure in whatever you might say. Here's a question for you. Should email be spelled e-mail or email?

Off to what I hope will be fun!

SPELLING WORDS ARE FOR THE BIRDS

I asked my teacher how to spell bird,

Next day she got mad when I wrote wird.

Then she sed, "Here's how you spell Word.

That's different from how you spell Bird!"

Last night I asked mom before going to bed,

"Mom, is this the right way to spell sed?"

My mom answered and she almost saw red,

"Ted, you've really got to learn how to spell said.

With our crazy spelling I've had enough,

Keeping spelling straight can be quite rough.

Why not spell enough- enuf,

And how would it hurt if we spelled rough- ruf?

The other day I went to the zu,
Through the gate I did go thru.
How about spelling it zu and thru?
The shirt we're wearing could be blu,
And why then couldn't to be tu?

Yes, 'tis true I need to read,
Or, should it be I nead to reed?
My spelling needs to get up to speed,
If ever I hope that I will leed!

Here are some words about which I'd like to pick a bone.
Why don't we just spell telephone-telefone?
How about spelling symphony-symfony?
We'd still enjoy Mozart's beautiful harmony!

Silent letters are oh, so wrong.
Here is the English for which I long-
When the word rong we have to rite,
To dump the "w" would be so bright!
I'd like to be thru spelling through
The way that I was taught to do!
To make our spelling easier would not hirt,
To this cause I'd give my shirt!

Let's spell words the way they're sed,
Then our spelling tests we would not dred.
To look up a word in the dictionary,
Would be so simple, nothing skary!

Silent letters would be all gawn,

Our spelling would enjoy a brand new dawn.

Reeding and riting would be so eazy,

Us kids would find it simple and breezy!

Next is just a short poem. I vacillated as to whether to include this poem but decided to do so because it appeals to my winsome spirit. I smile as I use the word winsome for it is new to me. I am so tempted to tell you what it means, but I shall resist. I challenge you to either know the meaning or to look it up. I get The Word of the Day from one of my favorite websites: www.Dictionary.com.

Now to the poem that I decided to include just for my fun—maybe for yours. This poem was an email that I sent to my two awesome grandchildren, Dave and Em. I was coming to Ohio to visit them and was joking with them about a planned Monopoly game. We enjoy teasing and joking with one another immensely. Here's the poem:

MONOPOLY

This is a note to Emma and Dave:

Next week you both must be brave.

You must not growl! You must not howl!

I will bring you each a crying towel!

During Monopoly try to grin,

For your grandpa surely will win!

So try to be nice and be polite,

Do not argue and do not fight!

In a sense I am tickled and amazed as I write these chapters. I am beginning to wonder if this is a poetry book or an autobiography. The answer is, and perhaps you'll confirm, it is a poetry book with a hefty amount of autobiography. These last two poems I never expected would appear in this book, but now I feel they absolutely belong. I'm not sure how to say this, but maybe you can look beyond the words. I love my poems and I want to share them with you. However, I want you to know the writer, too. I think poetry is better understood and far more interesting if you know the poet. Hope I am right!

Here comes a wonderful poem. It is about the Christmas present that I received from Dave and Emma in 2007. Perhaps I should mention that about the first of December Dave and Emma received a letter from a fellow named Elmer Elf. Elmer's return address was: 1000 Santa Claus Lane, North Pole. It warned them both that they'd better start treating their grandfather nicely if they expected to get any Christmas presents. I think that's a good introduction to the following poem.

MY BEST CHRISTMAS PRESENT

It is Christmas Day and I'm loving it,

In my daughter's living room I do sit.

Dave and Emma, my grandkids, are precious to me,

They fill my being with joy and with glee!

They set this box right on my lappy,

They both know how to make me happy.

I open the box with lots of zest,

This present surely will be the best!

Ted Lennox

Another box is tucked inside,

My present I guess they wanted to hide.

Four boxes later I think I've arrived,

What an adventure these kids have contrived!

In the fourth box I hear something rattle,

Getting this gift has been an exciting battle!

Here's my present- I've reached my goal.

In goes my hand and Wow! A LUMP OF COAL!

I laugh out loud in total delight,

They've made my day and my night.

They've filled my heart with such awesome love,

I feel they have been sent from Heaven above.

CHAPTER

9

FROM MY PALS
BOTH GUYS AND GALS

This chapter has a great flare of excitement for me. The reason is that these poems are written by friends, family, and students. I personally treasure each of them, and I hope you will find pleasure and joy in reading them.

The first poem is written by a friend of mine of 55 years. His name is Ralph Peabody and Del was his wife. They had a fabulous influence and fantastic impact upon my ENTIRE life. I dare not start because this would become too lengthy. Ralph and Del are responsible for my terrific career, my wonderful wife, and my fabulous family. I truly would like to tell you much more about them but it would be too lengthy. Ralph was a professor at the University of Pittsburgh for 25 years. Shortly after retiring he and Del moved to Sherwood Oaks, a marvelous retirement center near Pittsburgh. To announce their move he sent this great poem to family and friends. Needless to say it is a treasure to me.

Ted Lennox

A VERY MOVING EXPERIENCE

By Ralph Peabody

Amidst the crates, boxes, and bags,
Chaos reigns and energy lags.
As we try to fit years of accumulations
Into a future without tribulations.

Yes, we have moved to a new life-style
And are settling into our new domicile.
From Pittsburgh with its bustle of humanity
We have moved to a suburban retirement community.

Sherwood Oaks is where you can find us,
In a country setting without much fuss.
No eaves to clean or lawn to mow
Others do those chores, even shovel the snow.

Our life it seems will be increasing its pace.
As new activities and friends find their place.
Our excitement and joy are running high.
We have truly found our place under the sky.

The next poem is written by Manal. I have known Manal since she was five years old. First she was my student during 4th, 5th, and 6th grades. Then, I had the privilege of having her as a student again when she was in the 10th, 11th, and 12th grades.

As I write this she is going into her third year in college, studying to be a lawyer.

Manal wrote this poem when she was a tenth grader. I will let her poem speak for itself, but wouldn't it be so wonderful if we could all live in peace together.

WAR AND ACCOMPLISHMENTS

By Manal Nasser

For every trigger pulled
And every arrow shot
We can feel the pain
When others cannot.
And for every stab
We will regret
The peace
We couldn't get.

War is mostly about one thing
Which is greed
It's about what people want
And not what people need.

No one cares
About the feeling of shame
All they care about
Is who to blame

Ted Lennox

From the past, life wasn't simple
And we all knew it
And we found out that fighting
Didn't help us through it.

The present is no different
From the past
But if we work as a team
We can conquer our problems at last.

If everyone will search
Deep in their heart
We can become one
And not split apart.
We can work together
Till the very end
Such as one
And one's best friend.

We can surrender ourselves
To what is right
And conclude to the motto
"We will not fight"

The next poem is written by Laura White, a student of mine starting back in second grade. Margaret Navarro, my friend and colleague, had the joy of teaching Laura to read braille. Now she is a dynamic student at Oakland University. Laura wrote this poem during her freshman year. She and I hope that you enjoy it.

SENSING AUTUMN

By Laura E. White

Have you ever tried to chase a leaf?
They move faster than we walk.
Have you ever listened to the bees;
And their constant honey talk?

Have you noticed the wind rustling through the trees;
Or tasted the sweetness on the autumn breeze?
Have you smelled rain falling on grass;
Or touched the frost as it covers animal tracks?

Have you heard the sad song of crickets;
As their swamps and thickets become chilly and dark?
Have you watched the moon retreat in to the glistening aurora;
Or noticed the sun with its colorful aura?

Have you hummed to the song of wild jays;
Or enjoyed the twilight of shortening days?
Have you taken the time to appreciate what would have been;
Have you sensed autumn?

I now want to introduce a poem that comes straight from my heart. It is a poem which I have treasured for the past 27 years. It was written by my darling daughter Amy when she was ten years old - approximately. As my mind and heart start to flood with emotion, please let me tell you about what caused her to write such a wonderful poem. Notice the joy and humor in the poem and then note how Amy pulls it all together with such intimate feelings in the final stanza. It's simply a treasure for me.

We lived in a wonderful neighborhood in Wyandotte, Michigan. In fact, I used to say to Laura, "We didn't buy a house, we bought a neighborhood!"

For several years, until the kids became teenagers, several families in the neighborhood would get together and go through the area Christmas caroling—men, women, and children. It was one of the Christmas season highlights! You are now ready to enjoy and appreciate Amy's warm and touching poem about these events.

Let me pause just for a moment while I wipe the tears of intimacy from my eyes. Amy tugs at my heart every time I read this poem. Thank you, dear Amy!

SINGING CHRISTMAS CAROLS

By Amy Lennox

On Christmas Eve we bundle up,
And go out caro-ling,
Our neighbors shut their windows,
when they hear my family sing!

My voice is very beautiful,
I sing just like a bird,
But everybody drowns me out,
So I am barely heard!

Dad sings like a buffalo,

And mother like a moose,

My sister, Marla, sounds like breaking glass,

And on second thought,

My father sounds like a goose.

Some people come and greet us,

They bring cookies on a tray.

I think they give us cookies,

Just to make us go away!

Though our singing sounds so sour,

It sends shivers down my spine,

When we're caroling together,

There's no family as sweet as mine!

Somehow I have an urge to reintroduce this poem to you. In the first chapter I included the poem that I use to start many days. Then I followed with the second and last poem in Chapter One which was titled "REALITY" by Viola Lukaweicki. This poem has meant so much to me that I'm including it in this chapter as well. For me, and I speak only for me, it means so very much.

Ted Lennox

REALITY

By Viola Lukaweicke

My thoughts are very potent things,

They hem me in or give me wings!

My thoughts create, enslave, or free,

Enrich, or impoverish me!

My own thoughts make me glad or sad,

They choose, decide, for good or bad!

Whate're they be, is true for me,

My thoughts are my Reality!

The next poem was written by my friends Leigh Hunt and Jonathan Wahl. It was part of the 2005 calendar that they presented to their Aunt Nina. As you will probably recall Nina is a close friend of mine. We have, among other things, run together for 26 years. My wife Laura and I have been friends with Leigh and Jonathan for over twenty years.

In 2006 my grandson Dave and I had the happy fortune to spend a week with Leigh and Jonathan in their condominium in the great state of Vermont. Much of that week was spent climbing mountains, sleeping in a tent on the ground, and enjoying every step out on the Long Trail.

When we weren't going up and down mountains during that week, thanks to Dave - we were "camping" at Ben and Jerry's ice cream headquarters!

I simply cannot resist telling you one wonderful story about running with Nina. (By the way, is this a poetry book or is it an autobiography?) Believe it or not, in the state of Michigan there is a small town named Hell. In January, 1984, they held a 10 kilometer run. The snow was plentiful and the temperature was five degrees above zero. Nina and I were standing on the starting line getting ready to "run through Hell." Next to me stood a pleasant gentleman; he kindly said to me: "Tell your wife that you both should be careful out on those roads- it's slippery, there's lots of ice." I chuckled then and I'm chuckling now. I, with a tone of joy in my voice, replied: "My wife is at home, sitting in our living room, sipping coffee, and reading the newspaper." Please enjoy this wonderful little episode. Then, read and enjoy this sweet poem.

O MICHIGAN RUNNER

O Michigan runner, so true and trim and fleet,

With determined pace through sun, rain, and sleet,

How sure you are throughout the year,

From tape to tape, nary wind nor snow to fear,

O Michigan runner, an inspiration high

For family and friends to smile and sigh,

On misty morns and frosted planes,

You join the throng with steady gains,

How yet you pace to an inner drummer,

To soar and train in a verdant summer,

Now 'tis another year to toe the line,

O Michigan runner, you're true, you're our runner, you're our "Aunt Nine".

Ted Lennox

The last poem in this interesting chapter is written by Bahzad Ballout. Bah is presently a senior at Lincoln Park High School. He was a student of mine during his fourth, fifth, and sixth grade years. I still have the pleasure of spending time with Bah because on occasion I have the honor of subbing for my friend Kim Canzoneri - who is Bahzad's teacher. Here is a poem he wrote for his literature class.

FLIGHT OF THE SIGHTLESS

By Bahzad Ballout

The sun warms me up as I walk with my cane,

The twitters of the birds relieve my pain.

I wave hello as people pass me by,

Their voices like different colors portrayed in the sky.

Scents of flowers greet my nose,

A gardenia, a daisy, and a lovely rose.

Now it rains, and I taste some drops,

I hear a wing flap and my thought pattern stops.

The sound of a loud caw perks my ear,

It's a crow, a creature I do not fear.

It flies around me, going from left to right,

It moves up and down, bobbing like a kite.

If I could fly just like that bird,

I'd fly away from whispers and any unkind word.

People look at my form as they talk and gawk,

While I sing a song which they should not mock.

Another bird rose, its movements slow and soft,

The immaculate creature then sang and coughed.

My heart told me there was something wrong,

For the bird could not fly and changed its song.

The tune became sad, but still warm and pure.

I sighed in satisfaction as it gave me a cure.

One wing was broken, I suddenly knew,

Because its flight and song rang very blue.

Even though injured, the creature could fly,

So I know I could too, and now realize why.

I might be different, with my eyes closed to sight,

But I will go on and fight with all my might.

The final poem for this interesting chapter is a poem written by Megan Richardson, Nina's daughter. I have a super story to tell you about Megan. This event occurred about 30 years ago when Megan was about sixteen.

My family and I were visiting Nina and her family one Saturday afternoon. We were in the backyard enjoying swimming in the swimming pool. Megan got a telephone call from a young man, a friend about her age, who said he was planning to come over and would be there about five o'clock. The call came to Megan at approximately two o'clock. Megan came bouncing out to the backyard and with much enthusiasm announced that Kevin was coming over to visit. Then, she quipped, "Wow! I've got just three hours to lose thirty pounds."

I want to complete this chapter with a poem Megan wrote to her mother this past Mother's Day, May 2009.

Ted Lennox

DEAR MOM

I love your style,
I love your grace,
From all the running miles
To winning every race.

You've been a great mentor
And a loving mom
With your wonderful splendor
And your enthusiasm like a bomb.

I want to say thank-you,
I am truly blessed.
I have a great mom in you,
A great friend who's the best.

Love,
Megan

CHAPTER

10

OUR DANCE WITH ROMANCE

MARVELOUS WIFE

I really cannot tell you of the depth of my love,

Could you have been sent from Heaven above?

No man has had a more wonderful wife,

I want you know how much you've enriched my life!

Thanks for all you've been so far,

Thanks for all you currently are.

Thanks for all our future will hold,

You are more precious than silver and gold!!!!!

This poem was written for and given to Laura on one of our anniversaries.

When I first started to write this book, I had no idea that there would be a Chapter Nine and especially a Chapter Ten - "OUR DANCE WITH ROMANCE." My notion was that the poems you are reading were to be read only by my incredible wife, Laura. However, as I started writing the book and talked with Laura and Nina about this thrilling project, the desire to share Laura with each of you grew. Please read, enjoy, and get to know Laura and me a little better.

Because of what has occurred in my life in the past five months this chapter will be rather different than it would have been five months ago. In fact, because this chapter is now so emotional I will probably seek Nina's advice as to whether it should be included in this book. This chapter will be quite different from the first nine chapters. You will understand as you read. Throughout this book I have introduced most of the poems before you read them. However, for the next one I want to make comments following the poem.

LAURA'S LAST DAY

I brought her coffee as she lay in bed,
That's because I love her and my name is Ted,
She said, "good morning" in a pleasant voice,
Being pleasant was her normal choice!

In our motel to the restaurant we went,
An intimate hour is what we spent.
We both ate omelets, bacon, and toast,
Enjoying each other the very most.

To our daughter's house we merrily did drive,
Laura was happy and so alive!
We played cards with Emma and Dave,
Of this hour I can only rave!

Lunch as a family is what we had,
We were all happy and Laura was glad.
Then off to watch Emma's beautiful dance,
She would not have missed this wonderful chance!

Emma's dance - Laura loved it all,
My darling wife was having a ball.
This day on earth she said was great,
Her whole being was in such a glorious state!

Ted Lennox

Back at the house dinner was a sensation,
But it wasn't as good as the conversation.
She enjoyed herself from fruit to dessert,
With my awesome wife I did flirt!
Emma, Marla, Laura, and I,
After dinner to the backyard we did fly,
To do what precious Laura loved so much,
For planting flowers she had a fabulous touch!

Planting flowers for her was an art,
She did it with her hands, her head and her heart!
We dug and planted for about an hour,
Soon there'd be many a beautiful flower.

To the motel we did go back,
On the way we picked up a snack.
We ate, we talked, we shared our day.
For Laura, the day was great in every way!

We wrapped each other in our arms,
She filled me with her many charms,
We kissed good night with loads of love.
During the night she left for heaven above!

As you now know, I lost my darling Laura during the night on Mother's Day. I felt I should tell you about this sad scenario poetically. I went to her side that Sunday morning, coffee in hand, and I could not wake her. I ran hastily to the phone and called 911. Upon returning to her side I found her oxygen hose lying on the floor. Thus, she had been oxygen-less for who knows how long. Thanks for your sensitive and kind understanding. I will get back to this situation later. Let me move on to my next poem. I will get back to this situation later.

During February of 2003 Laura spent the month in Florida visiting friends and relatives. That month was ever so long for me. I missed her so very much. What follows is the poem I wrote to welcome her home. I think the words will speak for themselves.

LYRIC OF LOVE

I hope your trip was oh so great,
Welcome home my wonderful mate,
I loved each night when you did ring,
Hearing your voice so full of spring.

Talking of the beach from your sweet lip,
Made me feel part of your trip.
Your time with Vita sounds like a blast,
That week sounded like it went so fast.

You and Jo Ann had such a fine time,
The time with Marla must have been sublime.
Spending time with Betty sure was fun,
The friendship, the beach, and all that sun!

Your return makes you more precious than before,
I want to hold you as you come through the door.
Do you really know how much I care-
how Heavenly that our lives we share?

Your mind is so beautiful, brilliant, and sharp,

Conversing with you is music played on a harp.

Your spirit is positive, and helps me to grow,

I'd be far less without you, I want you to know.

Your body thrills me from head to floor,

There's not a spot I don't adore!

What I am saying to you, my love,

Is God has sent you from Heaven above.

OX OX OX OX OX OX OX OX OX OX OX

The next poem was written to Laura for our 44th Valentine's Day.

TO LAURA ON VALENTINE'S DAY

I love you a pound and a ton,

Life with you is always full of fun!

I love you, you are so sweet!

You've always swept me off my feet!

Whether you're at home or far away,

My mind is on you night and day!

On Laura's 70th birthday I took her out for breakfast. We used the Henry Ford Retirement Village transportation. Henry Ford Village in Dearborn, Michigan, is where we moved from our fabulous neighborhood in Wyandotte. I had planned ahead of time with the driver. Just as we got in the car, Pete said: "Now, Mr. Lennox, which White Castle did you want to go to?" I told Pete that it was in Lincoln Park. So for the next 20 minutes Laura is a bit suspicious wondering what was going on. As we turned on to Fort Street, all of a sudden it hit her. She intuitively realized and said, "Oh Ted! We're going to Fergie's Restaurant." She was right.

Fergie's held many good memories. We had eaten there for around forty years. Amy had her first job at Fergie's. Here is the poem I wrote for Laura and gave to her as we ate breakfast and shared memories.

TO LAURA

In sun, rain, or snow!

I shall always love you so!

As long as we're together,

Happiness is mine, in any weather!

At breakfast, dinner, or lunch!

I shall always love you a bunch!

Summer, spring, winter or fall,

Being married to you is truly a ball!

Sitting alone or in a crowd,

Of you I am forever proud.

And in our after-life,

Remember you are still my WIFE!

It is my desire to share with you the poem I wrote to Laura on our 43rd anniversary. But, dare I ask you to let me share one more charming story about my salubrious wife? I dare! (:-)

In 1989 Laura signed up to go for a ladies' weekend retreat in Ann Arbor. For the entire month before the retreat I unabashedly told everyone about her going, and that during that weekend I would keep the house lively with lady after lady. She left on a Friday afternoon in March. I came home from school just a little before six. I hopped off the bus and walked a half mile to our house. I was peacefully looking forward to a quiet evening. Shortly after I walked in the back door the front door bell rang. I approached the door rather amazed, wondering who it could possibly be. I opened the door and in rushed three nice ladies—within ten minutes there were eight <u>ladies</u> in my living room. All of them were wonderful friends of ours. My unbelievable, charming, humorous wife had set this up. Can you believe it! We had a most enjoyable evening, and all the ladies said good night about nine o'clock. What a wife! What a friend!

I am grateful to all of you for taking time to honor us by reading this fabulous episode. Now here's the poem I lovingly presented to Laura with flowers on our 43rd wedding anniversary. Enjoy!!!

NUMBER 43

I am proud that you are my wife!

You add so much to my wonderful life!

I am so proud to call you Dear,

Our marriage gets better year by year!

Five hundred sixteen months we've lived together,

It's fun with you no matter the weather.

The weeks equal twenty-two hundred and thirty-four,

I'm signing up for that many more!

Fifteen thousand seven hundred and five days—

I love you, Laura, in so many ways.

It's been three-hundred seventy-six thousand, nine hundred twenty hours,

I send my love with these flowers.

22,615,200 minutes filled with joy,

I'm so fortunate to be your chosen boy!

1,356,912,000 seconds worth of caring.

I am so glad this life we're sharing!

So! Forward we go with an adventurous heart,

Beginning each day with a fabulous start!

My last lyric about luscious, loving Laura is called, "AMPUTATION YET MOTIVATION." The first word in the title is metaphorically accurate. The third word is crucial but is not always accurate. However, I strive to make it so. Laura and I had several conversations pertaining to the possibility that one of us would pass away before the other. We both encouraged each other to continue to LIVE, to build on our marriage foundation that we had developed together. This I'm trying to do daily.

Read the following poem with sensitivity, understanding, and empathy. The preceding sentence is important to me so I just looked up the word EMPATHY in my BrailleNote dictionary. Here is the meaning: "Empathy: noun. The ability to understand and share the feelings of another." The word empathy is exactly what I want! Thanks! So please read with your heart!

Ted Lennox

AMPUTATION YET MOTIVATION

On Mother's Day my love Laura did die.

Many tears I shed for I do cry.

Half of me had to leave,

Believe me for this I certainly do grieve!

I feel just like I've been amputated,

This at times makes me so deflated.

She's not with me to live and love,

She's gone off to heaven above!

Laura and I talked about this event,

Knowing that one of us would eventually went!

We shared with each other our mutual desire,

That the one left behind would live with joy and fire!

Laura and I lived together as one,

We shared our lives and it was fun.

Almost 46 years our lives we did share,

For each other we truly, truly did care!

Thus I feel like half of me was amputated,

In honor of you, Laura I'll stay motivated.

I will not become a troglodyte,

I will continue to live a life of delight!

Each day to you I shall dedicate.

Thanks for the memories - they're oh so great!

I will try to live with zip and zest,

I promise I'll do my very best!

There is a line in the poem where I promise Laura that I will not become a troglodyte. I am a member of Dictionary.com, and every day I get The Word of the Day. Shortly after Laura's final but marvelous day, troglodyte was the word of the day. The word, like many words, has various meanings and nuances. The meaning in the poem is that I will not become a hermit or withdraw from living.

Again, I am grateful to you for sharing this important chapter with me. I will keep trying to stay motivated and I shall not become a <u>troglodyte.</u>

Here comes a poem that is a bit different. I had not planned to include it in this chapter. During the first few weeks after Laura left I received many beautiful and kindly messages. They came to me in braille, e-mail, phone, and in print. Each and every one meant plenty to me and they helped me immensely. In cases where a group sent me a booklet or a card which many had signed,

I answered them with the following poem. I included a tactile picture representing Laura and I holding hands. My poem and touch picture were attached to many bulletin boards. Again, my reason for sharing this short poem is to emphasize how important each message was that people sent to me. I have sent many more messages to those losing a loved one than ever in the past, and each word has been genuine.

Ted Lennox

YOUR THOUGHTS FOR ME

Your cards to me meant so very much,

My heart you know you really did touch.

To think you still remember me is hard to believe,

Your encouragement through this trying time has helped as I grieve!

Laura, my friend and loving wife,

Will be part of me for the rest of my life.

45 years, 6 months, 20 days, and 17 hours,

She filled my life with happiness and flowers!

One evening this past Fall, I was ambling down the hall on the way to the swimming pool. I was dreaming about Laura and wishing she were here to be part of this exciting new adventure - swimming - that I started on October first. My mind was on Laura, swimming, and water. Here, at least for me, is the animating and thrilling result. You will get a look-see into our awesome union.

H2o
LAURA + TED

We were married back in 1962,

Hydrogen and Oxygen, we became new!

A brand new compound we did brew,

It was far greater than a glob of glue!

Hydrogen we will think of as Laur,

Such an element I did so adore.

Oxygen we will let be Ted,

In '62 Laura agreed with him to wed!

Hydrogen and Oxygen they did unite,
Knowing their life would be a wonderful flight.
Laura was not hydrogen any more,
Oxygen Ted chose to ignore!

We were a compound united as one,
Living with each other and having fun.
No longer hydrogen was my love Laur,
And Ted was not oxygen anymore!

Hydrogen plus oxygen we did combine,
The liquid we got was truly divine.
The water that resulted was so sublime,
For 45.5 years we had a wonderful time!

Holy water is what we became,
I was her boy, she was my dame.
Hydrogen and oxygen we easily gave up-
Water was what filled our marriage cup.

Sometimes we'd be a luscious liquid,
And the water we were was oh so good!
At other times we'd be hard frozen ice,
Those times too were always so nice!

And then there were times we'd be nothing but steam,
I was her love, she was my dream!
Ice, liquid, or steam, whatever the weather,
All that did matter was that we were together!

We were no longer elements apart,

We were united heart-to-heart!

Hydrogen and oxygen were Laura and Ted,

They became water through marriage instead!

In fourteen hours my book will be sent to the Trafford Publishing Company. Yesterday I decided to add the poem, "DEAR MOM," to the end of Chapter Nine. I mentioned to Nina that we'd best get this manuscript in the mail or I'd keep adding poems. Then I told her about a poem that I had recently written telling Laura how much better I could have been and should have been as her friend and husband. I couldn't believe it when Nina encouraged me to add the upcoming poem.

Laura has been gone now for 390 days, and I think about how much, much better a husband I could have been. So the following poem is written to Laura as an apology for not being that much better a husband.

I WISH I HAD LOVED YOU BETTER

With you I often felt a union of delight.

I wish I had cultivated that feeling morning, noon, and night.

I could, I should, have loved you so much better.

It was my own limitations that did me fetter.

You used to tell me to change my shirt,

That was because it carried some dirt.

Or you'd say: "Change your pants- they have a stain."

Gratitude should have filled my brain.

Most of the time with anger I'd bubble,

I blamed you for causing me so much trouble.

Laura, dear, you were being nothing but kind,

I couldn't see my clothes because I am blind.

My thanks should have come from deep inside,

My shirt I should have changed with nothing but pride.

My pants should have been changed with much great joy,

Knowing you cared for me and I was your boy!

I wish we had talked more heart to heart,

I should have been far more involved in your works of art.

About your sculpting and painting we should have talked,

Support and interest should have come from me

as we sat and as we walked.

I wish we had chatted more about our life,

Sharing our joys, and helping with strife.

Encourage you I did, I think you'll agree,

I could have done better but only now that I see.

We talked about our thoughts, feelings, and desires!

They meant so much, they filled my being with fires!

But Laura, my darling, I would that we'd shared a great deal more.

To your ideas, your feelings, your questions I'd have opened my door.

Ted Lennox

Before we were married we'd walk down the street,
Holding hands and moving our feet.
After marriage, sitting in meetings side by side,
We should have held hands and our love never hide!

Sharing our feelings, our thinking, our goals,
I wish I had made that a big part of my roles.
I wish I had shared my love without fear,
More often called you darling, sweetheart, and dear!

Had only I surprised you with more flowers,
Brought them to you at unusual hours.
Then bring you a present every now and then,
How could I lose? I could only win!

I wish for you, once per week, I'd held your car door,
Not because I should, but to show how much you I adore!
And every day I wish I had given you a loving kiss,
To let you know you filled my life with bliss!

I wish, I wish, I wish, you get the gist,
I could go on and on with this never ending list.
I hope somehow you looked beyond my exterior,
'Cuz my love for you was so much superior.

You for me were the perfect gal,
You were my friend, you were my pal.
We weren't two people separate and apart.
We were connected heart to heart!

Not long after Laura departed I realized that she <u>was</u>, <u>is</u>, and <u>will be</u> an integral and vital part of my life day-in-and-day-out. She will always be with me to inspire, influence, and improve my life. Ergo, I wrote the following poem to her. The poem says it all, so I will not say more!

YOU CAN'T LEAVE ME

Darling, darling, Laura Lou,

Your days on earth will never be through!

You are with me day and night,

From this assignment there is no flight!

To bed we go every night,

Your pillow, darling, is still on my right.

You bring a book and turn on the light.

Lying beside you is such a delight!

At OUR bank they quietly shout,

Please take Laura off your bank account.

This request I really must flout,

To this concept I believe I will be stout!

Last week to church I went with Elaine and Bill.

I trudged through ice and snow and did not spill.

They wanted to know why I went behind the car,

Why not sit behind Elaine, that's not far?

But Laura, I would never take your seat,

Where would you put your fanny and your feet?

Ted Lennox

399,923 hours physically we lived as one.

You will always be part of me 'til my life is done.

Please remain in my heart embedded,

For you and I shall always be wedded!

Darling, darling, Laura Lou,

Your days on earth will <u>never</u> be through.

You are with me day and night,

From this assignment there is no flight!

CHAPTER

11

WE ARE NOW CAUGHT
WITH A LITTLE
AFTERTHOUGHT

About two weeks ago I was chatting with a friend in Duluth, Minnesota. I mentioned that if I don't move forward and get this book published I'd have to go back and insert several poems into different chapters. In fact, I already had six poems to insert, and I mentioned that I did not like the idea of changing any of the chapters. I told her that I was considering a Chapter Eleven and just putting together a potpourri of my additional poems. She encouraged me to do so and suggested that I might call the final Chapter, "AFTERTHOUGHTS;" since this is a poetry book I wanted each chapter title to be a bit poetic, thus the title, "WE ARE NOW CAUGHT WITH A LITTLE AFTERTHOUGHT."

During my finale as a teacher in 2003-2004 I did an amazing amount of reflecting. I looked back over my past seventy-one years and reflected upon those people who have had a MAJOR, POSITIVE, AWESOME, and INSPIRING influence on my life. I do not doubt that after this book is done I may write a poem about each of the following fantastic friends. I would like to go on and add a chapter twelve and pay a special tribute to each of them. Because I have set a firm goal to have this book published by April 30 I shall resist the temptation. I am introducing each person in chronological order.

1. My two brothers Frank and Cecil included me in all neighborhood activities - baseball, skiing, biking, golfing, on and on.

2. Richard and Robert Tenniswood were like brothers to me in the years that I attended The Michigan School for the Blind in Lansing and lived in the dorm. Richard and Robert were twins. They had some vision and thus surreptitiously we had an automobile hidden by the railroad tracks behind the school. They did have driver's licenses. Lavern Little was also a friend at MSB.

3. Mac Lott was my faithful friend and college roommate for three years at Michigan State. Mac showed me how to get from Phillips, our dorm, to East Mayo Hall so I could hold my head high and surprise my first date by picking her up at her dorm.

4. "Stony", real name Mary Adams, is a girl I met at Michigan State. She read to me and we became friends. In fact, we took two classes together with the agreement that we'd both get A's. We did! She lived in East Mayo dorm. You figure it out!

5. Jan Berry, "Toot", is another girl who read to me. We developed a flourishing friendship. During the spring term we went to lunch together every Tuesday. I called those lunches romantically Tuesdays with Toot!

6. Ralph and Del Peabody were two people who made my entire adult life a dream come true. I met Ralph at Michigan State in a Physiology class.

7. Laura-lou, (guess who?) I also met at Michigan State, and I dare not say more or this book would not end.

8. Nina Derda- as you know, we've been through Hell together!! (Check out Chapter Nine, just before the poem, "O MICHIGAN RUNNER." (:-) (:-)

9. Margaret Navarro, with whom I taught side by side for 30 years, I frequently called my second wife. (:-) She and Laura were good friends and they'd laughingly comment that I'd better not get them mixed up!

10. Bob Voulemenous, my friend and neighbor, was a running partner for 30 years. When he and Val moved into our neighborhood he'd wave to me every morning as he drove to work. He thought I was unfriendly because I never waved back!!! We shared so much during our hours of running.

11. John Whitacre and I have taught computer camps together for the last twelve years. Team teaching with John is exhilarating and we have developed a close friendship.

The upcoming poem is dedicated to each of the above <u>inspiring, dear friends</u>. Please know that the words represent a profound truth. I just hope that each of them know how sincere and serious this poem is.

FROM MY HEART TO YOURS

I wish I had the words to say

The thoughts and <u>feelings</u> I'd like to convey,

But there's no way that I can start

To tell you what resides in my heart!

Ted Lennox

Let me get this off my chest,

You've helped me to be my very best!

Thank you for opening the door of love,

You surely were sent from Heaven above!

These are feelings I want to share,

Coming from my heart I want to declare.

In 1981 when I started running, I would run around our block. The distance was three-tenths of a mile. In order to protect my body I put a pleasant note into every mail box asking my neighbors to be sure not to park across the public sidewalk. It worked very well, except—I overlooked putting my letter in one mailbox. So one Saturday afternoon I was out for a 5-mile run and all of a sudden - unexpectedly - I ran smack dab into a solid van. Guess who inadvertently parked across the public sidewalk? I picked myself up, went in the house and kissed the owner of the van.

I laughed right after the comical collision and I'm laughing joyously now as I write this.

Off to the poem.

I SEE WITH MY FEET

I wear heel plates on my shoes,

About the environment they give me clues,.

The sound waves they send are sharp and clear,

They tell me accurately if anything's near!

I walk down the sidewalk very brisk,

Will I run into something? Not much of a risk.

Information about what's ahead of me I do not lack,

My heel plates send sound waves and I get the feedback!

Across the sidewalk a person may park their car,

I speed ahead, I don't fear a scar.

My heel plates send sounds that bounce back to my ear,

I walk confidently with nothing to fear!

I walk down the hall at the high school with class,

Listening to the sound of each door as I pass.

Room 109 is the door that I seek,

I listen to the sound waves and they are not weak!

When coming home I want to turn on my street,

There's a tree at the corner that I'm eager to greet.

The heel plates that are attached to the bottom of my feet

Will tell me when that tree I do meet!

The sound of the tree speaks directly to me

And I make a left turn so easily.

For me each shoe must have a heel plate,

The resounding sound is so very great!

We all live in two worlds. There is the outer world that consists of other people, trees, houses, and so forth. Our outer world includes everything outside of us.

The other world is our inner world. Our inner world is the more important one. It is made up of our thoughts, our feelings, and our behavior. Our inner world is so vital to our happiness and our confidence. Yet, it is the world to which many of us pay the least attention. We tend to focus on our outer world, letting what happens in the outer world determine how we feel and how we think. Our focus, our effort, our energy should be on developing our own inner world. It's the inner world where we need to be in charge. In fact, is there anything more important for any of us than that of developing a positive, happy, confident inner world? Let's let the next poem speak to this powerful premise.

PLANT THOSE SEEDS, CLEAR THOSE WEEDS

We each have a garden called our mind,

Do we grow flowers, or do we grow weeds?

What kind of growth in it do we find?

It is important to plant the right seeds!

Plant positive seeds that create happiness,

Our personal garden we should all fertilize.

With negative seeds we should never mess,

This each of us we should emphasize!

Our garden, the mind, we should constantly hoe,

Pull those weeds, negative thoughts, don't let them grow.

Hoe your mind both night and day,

Keep your garden beautiful in every way!

Watch your soil- be constantly alert,

Keep it rich and free from dirt.

If a negative thought in your mind should appear,

Send it away and your mind do clear.

Here's what you can do to clear the dirt,

A positive thought in it's place please insert!

So whenever you think a negative weed,

Insert a positive seed indeed!

So, make each thought a beautiful flower,

Monitor your thoughts hour by hour,

Weed your garden all the while,

Plant only seeds that make you smile!

For the past little while I have been searching for and seeking this upcoming poem because it is such an important one. I was struggling to find where in the devil I had saved this powerful poem. Finally, I found it hidden in a folder on my PC drive. Take a wild guess as to what you think is the name and the subject. The poem is called, "ORGANIZE." You'll undoubtedly concur with me that I need this poem badly.

Please notice that it is written from the point of view of anybody. For instance, I talk about losing my car keys. As you know, I don't drive or, more accurately, Laura and I don't tell others when I drive! When Marla was four and Amy one, we were visiting Laura's brothers. They lived out in the country on rarely traveled dirt roads. Laura suggested that I might want to drive because it would be perfectly safe. Of course, I jumped at the chance! The only thing was that Marla refused to ride with her daddy. She rode with her uncle instead. Amy didn't seem to mind!

Here is this powerful poem!

Ted Lennox

ORGANIZE

Where, oh where, are my car keys,
Tell me, tell me, if you please.
Where could they be, oh golly jeeze!
Here they are behind the cheese!

My glasses- I had them a moment ago.
Someone moved them, that I know!
Oh! here they are on the bathroom sink.
Why were they there? Let me think!

I wonder where I put my book,
By the bed let me look!
Where in the devil could that book be?
Oh! here on the porch by the settee!

My credit card- I hope it's not lost!
If someone's got it, it really could cost!
It's driving me nuts, where could it lay?
Right here- behind the toaster you say!

I just got a check from my friend Elaine,
Where did I put it, what a pain.
I've looked everywhere, let me think,
In the laundry basket, under the sink?

Is it sitting on top of the TV?
Or out in the yard under the tree?
Oh! Here it is by the outgoing trash,
I almost lost some important cash!

I just brought in today's new mail,
I'm sure I put it away without fail!
Well, let me take time to retrace my trail,
Whoops! Here it is beside the garbage pail!

Now, where did I put the IRS form?
I'm searching the house- am I getting warm?
For this form I'm really itchin'.
Hot dog! I found it here in the kitchen!

The day is cold, my hands are froze,
The wind is biting at my nose.
My gloves, my gloves, where did they hide!
It's ten degrees and I'm working outside!

The day is now over and I'm home to doze,
My fingers all day have been terribly froze.
I'll find my gloves sometime later,
Oh no! Here they are in the refrigerator!

I guess there's something I should recognize,
So many benefits when I think to organize.
Always put the keys in my pocket or purse,
To lay them around, what could be worse?

Ted Lennox

My glasses should be around my neck,
I'd never lose them, what to heck!
Where they'd be would not be a worry,
It would save plenty of hurry and scurry!

My book should go into the book case,
Then, my book, I'd never have to chase,
It would always be in its proper place,
And I would have a smile on my face!

My credit card is like silver and gold,
Why don't I keep it in my billfold?
Just to lay it around willy-nilly,
That's so dangerous and so-so silly!

With cash and checks- be a bit bolder,
Put them aside in a special folder!
Don't lay them down helter-skelter,
Put them in a definite shelter.

Have a location for incoming mail,
Put it there right away without fail.
Who cares if it's in print or braille,
By losing it you might end up in jail!

I must find that form from the IRS,
If I don't, I'm in a big, big mess.
Here it is right under the table,
Oh to be organized, I wish I were able!

I think my gloves should consistently reside

In my coat pocket, where they can't hide.

Then, as I step out into the frost,

I'll have my gloves, they won't be lost!

As I write this poem I do realize

It's extremely important to organize.

It saves time and futile frustration,

The above examples are a good illustration!

A couple of weeks after Laura Lou passed away my daughter Amy read me a meaningful little book, "THE PRECIOUS PRESENT." Spencer Johnson. Spencer's idea is that we all have a present, and that present is the present. His theme is that we, each of us, you and I should enjoy and thrive with this present, the present- another stimulating metaphor and worthy of attention.

Amy presented this concept most effectively at Laura's Memorial Service which later motivated me to write this poem.

THE PRECIOUS PRESENT

I want to share with you a present.

This present for us both is so so pleasant.

Neither of us should put it in a book case,

It should accompany us with our every pace!

It's easy to overlook this wonderful gift,

An ongoing gift that will give us a lift.

We need to keep it ever in mind,

It's a present we <u>never</u> need find.

What is this present you may inquire?

What is the gift that can set us on fire,

What is this present that you and I share?

It's always here, it is not rare!

This present that each of us may use

Is <u>this moment</u> that we should choose.

The present we each have is THE PRESENT.

Enjoy it! Keep it ever so pleasant!

You probably know I promised Laura that if she went first I'd continue to live, and that I would not permit myself to become a <u>troglodyte.</u> That was a serious promise, quite different from the promise I made Laura when I proposed. I've documented that marriage promise near the end of Chapter One. The following poem was written to motivate and encourage myself.

I TRY TO BE BAD

I need to confess that I am really BAD.

Shame on me, for that makes me glad!

May I explain this to you, my comrade?

Maybe you won't feel that I'm such a bad lad!

The letter B stands for the word BOLD.

I want to be bold whether young or old.

Bold is the way I want to feel inside,

Help me, God, this trait never to hide!

Adventure is represented by the letter A.

Dear God, help me live adventurously each day.

May I keep trying new things, all the while

Enjoying each adventure with a smile!

Living a daring life is the way I want to exist.

Dear God, help me, help me not to resist!

On living this style of life I will try to insist.

To be daring each day I will endeavor to persist!

BOLD is the way I'm determined to think.

ADVENTURESOME the flavor of life I'll drink.

DARING, that's the kind of guy you'll see.

BAD is what I've decided to be!

The upcoming poem belongs in Chapter Six, "REFLECTING, RESPECTING, CONNECTING." However, since it has recently been written I include it in this chapter. As you will see, it is a metaphor comparing our minds to a house. It's a challenge I take on daily.

Ted Lennox

REMODELING THE MIND

I shall pretend that my mind is a home,
From room to room I shall now roam.
I shall remodel and redecorate
My home I will aim to make first-rate!

I have to remodel my mind 'tis true,
And boy! I have a lot of work to do!
I think I'll do it thought by thought,
So much defective thinking myself I have taught!

I will remodel my thinking from dull to bright,
I'll monitor my thoughts through day and night.
If a negative thought takes up mind-space,
I'll put a positive thought in its place!

Eliminating negative thinking is an exciting job,
I have discovered that there is quite a mob.
Positive thinking I'll substitute instead,
With positive thoughts I will fill my head!

Let me start first with my living room.
The furniture there are thoughts about me.
There are many limiting thoughts, they're
full of gloom.
I'll throw out the furniture with a feeling of glee.

My new furniture is now on display,
I set no limits, what a relief!
I will enjoy each and every day,
My furniture expresses positive belief.

Now into the kitchen of my mind,
What I cook there will be interesting to find.
Oh! Here are thoughts about my husband or wife,
About him or her, negative thoughts cause such strife.
My mind kitchen I will redecorate until bright,
I will perceive my spouse in nothing but sunny light!

I go now into my cluttered den.
I'll get rid of negative thoughts about others,
But where, oh where, should I begin?
Remodel those thoughts about family, friends, and brothers!

Think thoughts that express total respect,
Then watch and see what a fabulous effect.
Allow thoughts in your den that only project
Thoughts of acceptance not thoughts that reject!

Let me complete my house metaphor,
I'm remodeling my mind from ceiling to floor.
This type of adventure is an architectural thrill,
Remodeling my mind will help my life to fulfill.

Ted Lennox

Here comes an important poem because of the awareness it created within me. For most people, seeing is the major way they experience the world. For me hearing and touching are my highways to experiencing and knowing the world. Jan, also known as "Toot", brought this to my awareness when we were in college in 1955. Her brief comment and support brought this important insight into my mind because of the exhilarating experience I had with her at that time.

I SEE WITH MY FINGERS

I once had a super good friend,

Her name was Jan, but I called her Toot.

She stimulated my thinking, what an awesome trend,

The thinking she inspired bore lots of fruit.

In college I was exploring items in her dormitory room,

We were talking and laughing, there was not any gloom.

A friend whose name was Jane was present.

Jane was lively and always so pleasant.

At a point she expressed in a joyful tone,

Ted's fingers are busy; he leaves nothing alone.

Toot replied, and she did not linger,

That's because Ted sees with his finger!

In many respects my fingers are my eyes,

Touching things to understanding gives rise!

I love my fingers, I love my hand,

They add meaning to life and that is grand,

I see with my fingers night and day,

Toot brought that to my attention in a positive way!

If you are blind, then your fingers are your eyes.

She upped my awareness, it was a wonderful surprise!

There are three aspects to the next poem which I'd like to mention before you read it. First, when I read it I am swamped with such soothing and touching feelings. Second is the humor which I want you to interpret. Third, note the absolute joy Laura and I shared. February 10, 1967. What a night!

MARLA'S DEBUT

It was Thursday night about 10:00 PM.

Laura said, "Get ready! Will it be a her or a him?"

We were about to have our baby – oh, what a joy!

Will it be a girl or will it be a boy?

I knew that I certainly dare not drive,

We had to keep our baby alive!

I picked up the phone and I did not stop,

I called the police because I needed a cop!

In a matter of minutes two policemen arrived.

They, too, wanted our baby to be born alive.

They said, "I'm glad to your baby you are being kind.

You shouldn't drive to the hospital if you are blind."

As Marla grew up and became aware,
She often to me, her dad, would declare,
"Thanks for calling the police, dear Dad.
Had you done the driving it would have been sad."

I sat all night out in the hall,
Wondering if Laura was having a ball!
It was at 6:20 AM that Marla appeared,
Out of Laura's body she now had cleared.

I touched Marla's skin and held Laura's hand,
The feeling inside me was oh! so grand.
What a wonderful adventure lay ahead!
I'll treasure them both until I'm dead!

How about a poem introducing you a little further to my daughter, Amy? The next poem tells about an incident that took place in 1974. She was a sweet four-year old. This incident tells you a bit about Amy's sense of humor. One evening the four of us were at the kitchen table eating dinner. Amy offered to pour me a glass of milk and I accepted happily and innocently. Read the poem and use those fourteen muscles that it takes to smile and laugh.

EATING WITH MY FAMILY

We're sitting at the table eating dinner,
With Laura's cooking it's hard to stay thinner.
My daughters both are happily giggling,
I don't know if they are eating or wiggling!

Amy, who now has reached age four,

With a sense of humor I so adore,

Pleasantly pours me some liquid to drink,

It's milk, at least that's what I think.

I hoist the glass up to my lip,

Then, I take an ample sip.

The liquid hits my tongue with a bang,

It's as if a loud siren inside me has rang!

You'll never guess what she poured in my glass.

It was vinegar! And wow, was it sour!

The laughter it caused was really first class,

I must have laughed for up to an hour!

Every Sunday for the past two years I've been getting this wonderful newsletter called Increase Brain Power. I can't say enough good things about it and how important it has become in my life. For those interested, the address to Steve Gilman's website is www.increasebrainpower.com. What follows is both a cute and a positive message, I hope. The poem below came about because of an item he introduced me to a few weeks ago. I loved it then and I love it now. I wish I had the time to tell you the beautiful story as to how I, after so many years, learned what the face looks like while smiling.

Ted Lennox

SMILE OR FROWN

It takes just fourteen muscles to smile,
Without getting tired you can smile quite a while!
We can smile and do it with eloquent ease,
Smiling is simply a relaxing breeze!

It takes forty three muscles for you to frown.
Frowning does nothing but take you down.
Use those fourteen muscles and smile to success.
Using forty three muscles to frown creates a mess!

Maybe some people think it makes them strong and fit,
But probably this notion is that of a nit-wit! Frowning away all day long,
Maybe they think they're building muscles strong,
But I would suggest that they are wrong!

Build your body and keep it well,
You will feel happy and really swell.
Keep your body oh so healthy,
That's better than being rich and wealthy!

Just use those fourteen muscles all through the day,
Happy you'll be in every way.
Smile away and do not frown,
You'll be exuberant, you won't feel down!

I am endeavoring to end this exciting poetry book, exciting to me, not necessarily to anyone else, however I keep adding additional poems. Here's what I shall try to do- complete this book with the upcoming poem. It will be followed by my wish for both you and me.

The poem is a bit unusual in that it starts talking about my wrestling career but then goes on to propose a significant and important idea for me at least.

Before parading this poem by you I need to talk about my wrestling career and share a pleasant memory. First, externally I was not a great wrestler, just so-so. My won-lost record throughout high school and college was about fifty-fifty. Having told you that, now I can comfortably share this meaningful memory.

During my sophomore year in college at Michigan State all of my opponents would kindly keep in contact. That is, they would be sure that either I was touching them or they me. However, along came my junior year and I discovered that they no longer felt contact was necessary or wise. It was up to me to get hold of them and keep hold. My interpretation of the change was that their respect for me had grown to the point that it was up to me to tie up with them.

This, my final poem, means much to me. It starts out talking about one important aspect of my young life and ends up with a broad and beautiful notion, for me, about living a lively life in <u>all</u> areas.

THE UNDEFEATED WRESTLER

I was fourteen and in ninth grade,
The wrestling team I easily made.
I started wrestling at 95 pounds,
My opponents and I enjoyed all of our rounds!

Ted Lennox

All through high school I wrestled with zip,
I grabbed my opponents with a manly grip.
My opponents and I we gave our best,
We allowed each other no time to rest.

To Michigan State I went with fear,
But I made the team my sophomore year.
Three breathtaking years I wrestled for the green and white,
My matches were wrestling- they were never a <u>fight</u>.

I wish I had learned to follow this thought-
We are free to have two kinds of personal success.
It is with internal success that our minds should be caught,
If so, with external success we need not mess!

Much of the above is full of baloney,
So help me to cease being such a phony.
Confidence is what I always did lack,
Let me share my thinking if I could only go back!

I would not focus on winning or losing,
Simply to enjoy wrestling would be my choosing.
Each moment would be a special treat,
I wouldn't care if I won or got beat!

I would play the game with a joyful smile,
Enjoying my opponent all the while.
Be that the case, when I stepped on the mat,
I'd be a winner, and that would be that!

My internal world I should not overlook,

Whether wrestling a match or reading a book.

Internal success should be a constant part

Of my thinking and feeling, it should come from the heart!

Thanks for letting me share myself so openly and honestly.

Now for my final thought and message to you.

To your future and to mine,
May each moment be divine!

THE AUTHOR

SNEAK A PEEK

I popped into the world in 1933,
Born in the back of our drugstore – just believe me.
Since then and right up to now part of my life's scheme
Is that I enjoy and relish eating ice cream!

At age five, I my family left.
My heart, my heart it became bereft.
Back in those days if you could not see,
You left home and to school you had to flee!

While in school I participated in many-a-sport,
Baseball, basketball, football and more I'm happy to report.
At Michigan State I wrestled, I was not great.
One hundred fifty-seven was my wrestling weight!

Thanks to my good, good friends Ralph and Del,
I had a teaching career that was oh so swell.
Forty-eight years was my career duration,
Every day was a wonderful sensation!
It was at Michigan State I met my wife Laur,

During college, a degree, a wife- who could ask for more!

My wife, Laura, I simply adore.

Living with her, my life could not be a bore!

Marla and Amy are our daughters supreme,

For both Laura and I they fulfilled our dream.

They've added to our life a special note,

Marla and Amy, you get our vote!

If you read this book, please don't hesitate.

A message from you would be so great!

I promise I will reply within a week.

Thanks for taking this little peek!

tedlennox@gmail.com